LIFE! BY DESIGN

LIFE!

BY DESIGN

6

**Steps to an
Extraordinary
You**

TOM FERRY

WITH LAURA MORTON

Ballantine Books 🏛 New York

Published in the United States by Ballantine Books, an imprint of The Random House Publishing Group, a division of Random House, Inc., New York

Ballantine and colophon are registered trademarks of Random House, Inc.

ISBN 978-0-345-52064-7

Printed in the United States of America on acid-free paper

www.ballantinebooks.com

2 4 6 8 9 7 5 3 1

First Edition

Book design by Diane Hobbing

*I want to dedicate this book to my wife, Kathy, for saying yes
and continuing to be a yes throughout our marriage*

To my sons, Michael and Steven

And to all of you who will choose to live your life By Design

CONTENTS

INTRODUCTION

As a success coach, I think of myself as a life strategist in a business world. I travel from city to city giving lectures and conducting seminars that help change people's lives. Often while giving these talks, I'll lock eyes with someone in the audience I sense is in need of special attention, someone who's reacting strongly—but not necessarily *happily*—to my message. There's a look people get when they're hearing things, often for the first time, that tap into fears they've been struggling to keep at bay, and when I see that expression of panic or desperation, I try to connect to it, to help draw it out.

A few years back I noticed a woman—I'll call her Mary—sobbing throughout one of my presentations. What I found strange was that this particular event was an uplifting and inspirational sales training course, so her emotional response seemed quite out of the ordinary. My workshops are often designed to evoke a fervent response from the participants—to upset their applecart—but this wasn't one of those times.

During our first break, I decided to look for Mary to make sure she was okay. When I found her, I asked what was wrong. It didn't require much more of a push than that to get her to tell me.

"I'm the number one real estate salesperson in my company and number sixteen in the country," she explained. "But my 'all-business' approach is taking its toll on every other area of my life. I don't know what to do."

I'd heard this story many times before, so I asked her some pointed questions.

"Are you married or single?" I'd barely spoken the words when she began to cry again. I took her tears to mean she was married . . . but maybe not for long.

"Do you have kids?" Her sobs now became loud wails as she spoke about her three-year-old daughter and nine-year-old son.

"Are you with them as often as you'd like?" Not surprisingly, this question nearly brought her to her knees.

"I feel as if I hardly know my own children!"

The pain, guilt, and anguish she was feeling about how out of balance her life had become was palpable; clearly, she had hit a wall. There was no question the woman knew how to be successful in *business,* but she didn't have a clue about how to be successful in *life.* She had put all of her eggs in her career basket, and now everything else was suffering. What happened? How did she get here?

For much of my professional life, I've worked as a success coach to individuals and corporations specializing in sales and marketing. I help people like Mary become more successful in their chosen field, while simultaneously achieving a better balance across all the key areas of their lives. That's what I do, and that's why I've been invited to speak to dozens of leading corporations and have served as head coach to hundreds of top executives over the past twenty years.

After my conversation with Mary, I agreed to take her on as a client, to help coach her through this tough transition in her life. But first I needed her to agree that she would make whatever adjustments I asked of her. She quickly got on board without hesitation.

A week later, Mary had her first coaching session. I asked her to tell me more about her business.

"I'm the 'open house' queen of my town," she said.

Okay, I thought. Stop right there.

Many of my clients have worked in real estate, an arena with which I am extremely familiar. So I knew that if Mary held open houses as often as she said, she spent all of her weekends selling real estate—and none at home with her family. Her kids were in school and her husband worked Monday through Friday. I asked her what days *she* worked.

"Monday through Sunday."

This was the answer I'd feared, and expected. She worked virtually all the time. Most importantly, she hadn't been able, or willing, to be home on the weekends with her family.

"And how is *that* working for you?" I asked with my tongue firmly planted in my cheek, knowing full well it wasn't working for her at all.

It was obvious that every choice she made had driven her to incredible levels of success in her business but had also pushed her personal life into a state of crisis. Most of us overcompensate in one area of our lives as a way of masking problems in other areas. I have dozens of clients who throw themselves into work as a way of avoiding dealing with troubles in other aspects of their lives, such as their marriage, relationships, finances, and health. When I ask if they know why they do that, most of them come back with some excuse or another, but never a valid reason.

But there is a reason; there's always a reason. For most of us, it's easier—or we *imagine* it's easier—to keep slogging forward on autopilot, what I call living *by default*, than to ask ourselves the hard questions and make the necessary changes to live *By Design*. Living by default means *choosing* to live with pain and disappointment, falling short of our potential in every area of our lives.

Why do we choose this? Is being stagnant really easier than facing change? When you think about it, how easy is it to deal with daily struggle, self-pity, and failure?

Here's the thing. To achieve real change and growth, you have to decide what you're *not* taking responsibility for in life.

What are you avoiding?

For some of us it's pain—and for others intimacy. Maybe you feel lost, bored, or unchallenged at work. Perhaps you're afraid of change or have become so comfortable in your present state that any thought of disturbing your seemingly peaceful existence scares you to death. Whatever your reasons, it's time to call out the white elephant, assume responsibility, make some new choices, and then take action.

To test Mary's commitment, I asked if she'd be willing to cancel all of her open houses for the upcoming weekend and create a different approach to being a mother and a wife.

She began to cry because, although my suggestion was a simple one, it represented an entirely different way of life for her. But it was clear she wanted to try, so I gave her an immediate task.

"I want you to go buy the strongest sunblock you can find, grab your kids, and head to the beach." I told her to keep driving west until she saw the infinite blue Pacific in front of her. She was taking notes furiously as I spoke.

"Pack a picnic lunch. Got it.

"Bury the kids in the sand. Got it.

"Toss the Frisbee. Got it."

Yup. She was taking notes on how best to ensure a day of fun at the beach with her kids. That's how bad it had gotten for Mary, and how desperately important it was to her that she get it right.

And boy did she ever. Sixty days after that first conversation, her marriage was back on track, and she had become an extraordinary hands-on mother who spent more time with her children, made them dinner, and even helped them do their homework. And as happy as she was about this outcome, she was just as astonished to discover that her sales had actually gone *up* at work. By choosing to work fewer hours, she was forced to be more efficient. As a result she became the number-ten-ranked real estate agent in the country (up from number sixteen) by taking more weekends off!

We completely shifted how she operated in her life.

How did we accomplish this? What was the process by which Mary came to recognize that she'd been living by default? How did she face her fears, assess and reorient her priorities, and manage to get everything she wanted? This—learning how *you* can live life *By Design*—is the subject of my book.

What if I told you that in the midst of tough economic times my business is growing; I've been happily married for seventeen years and counting; I'm connected with my two boys—Michael, age eleven, and Steven, nine; I have an active social life; I'm physically fit; and, most important, I'm happy? Is it possible during challenging times to be this way? I say yes! I simply decided a long time ago to live By Design, no matter what else is happening in the world, including crumbling financial markets, plummeting real estate values, and other outside events we all deal with every day.

Now, what if I told you I could help you achieve the same results in your own life—show you how to navigate the rough water we all tread—by creating a plan to not only survive but actually thrive in difficult times?

Would you want to know more?

Great.

Then let's get started.

When I meet new clients, our first conversation is always about their family. I want to know everything about their upbringing, childhood, parents, siblings, and current personal life because I believe the best way to get to know someone is to fully understand where they come from. I ask about traumatic moments, deep dark secrets they've never shared, and any other indicator to help me understand who I am talking with. Personal history is an excellent gauge of how we all choose to live our daily lives as adults. All of our emotional baggage, hang-ups, and self-imposed roadblocks are tied to events and stories we tell ourselves from the past. The biggest problem for most people is that the past is where they choose to spend most of their energy, time, and thinking. They're stuck and unsure of how to get out from under all of that history. Does this sound familiar?

You might be asking yourself, What does this guy know about hardship, tough times, and turning around *my* life? Fair enough. These are legitimate and reasonable questions. After all, I'm not Dr. Phil. I don't have any letters following my last name, and, for some, this may be the first time you've heard of Tom Ferry. Because I believe that turnabout is fair play, allow me to tell you a little bit about where I come from and my background that got me where I am today.

My father was and still is a tremendously ambitious man. His parents were alcoholics for most of their lives. Although Dad always said he doesn't have a single memory before the age of nine, I am certain his early childhood must have been filled with trauma, drama, and unspeakable experiences.

Dad's family moved to Southern California when he was three years old. Dad developed an aggressive "get them before they can get me" attitude, which was common to his generation.

Mom was a beautiful, earthy, grounded caretaker who encouraged Dad to pursue his dreams while she dutifully stayed home, kept the house clean, raised their children, and held lovely dinner parties.

Ten years and four kids later, my parents divorced. I was just six years old.

Mom found work as a graphic designer so she could provide for us kids. Dad was building what would become a very successful business, but at the time, he was still scraping by.

Mom's two brothers, Kevin and Jeff, became father figures to my brothers, sister, and me because our dad was busy traveling for his business. We rarely saw Dad because he was on the road, sometimes as much as three hundred days a year.

Although I had a happy childhood after my parents divorced—there was always a lot of love and support at home—all of that changed one day when a new level of discipline entered our lives. Although Mom had dated on and off for about six years, life as we knew it was over when she met Pete, her knight in shining armor, who quickly threw down the proverbial gauntlet to let us know that he was now in charge. I was twelve years old when Mom met Pete. By this time, my older brother and I were running wild. I would stay out late and cut classes the next day, and had pretty much become a prepubescent punk. I'm sure my behavior caused Mom a lot of grief and heartache.

By the time I was thirteen years old, I had been exposed to drugs and alcohol. I started acting out for pure shock value. I grew my usually reddish brown hair long and dyed it jet black, a harsh look for a guy with fair skin. When I wanted even more attention, I'd use a lot of gel and wear my hair in a giant Mohawk. I slowly slid into a life I didn't expect.

I was often partying, going to local punk rock shows, and staying out late. I began lying to my parents about everything all the time. I partied as a way to escape my home life, which had become unbearable under Pete's steel fist and his constant prodding of my mother to get tougher with us kids.

By my fourteenth birthday, my partying was out of control. Even though I was one of the smartest kids in my class, I always came home with F's on my report card because I was bored by school. Nothing seemed to engage me except music, girls, and partying.

Mom and Dad were at their wits' end when they decided to send me to a "camp" in Idaho during the summer between eighth and ninth grade. Although camp may have been appealing to many kids my age, it was the last thing I wanted to do. I had conjured up thoughts of canoeing and tennis—hardly the way I was living my life. When Mom explained that she and Dad had already signed the waivers and permission forms, I quickly realized that my summer wasn't going to be one of leisure. Outward Bound was for candy-asses compared to Sioux Survival Camp, the twenty-one-day rehabilitation program that was my destination.

Two days before I left for camp, I hatched the perfect plan to run away as soon as I got there. I pretended that going away was no big deal. The night before I left, I dyed my hair with a fresh coat of black coloring to let everyone know I was a real badass. The next day I flew by myself to Boise, Idaho, where the camp supervisor met me and drove me an additional eighty miles to the camp. I was greeted by a tough-looking guy holding a clipboard; he welcomed me with a strip search. He immediately took away almost everything I'd brought, leaving me with one pair of socks, a pair of slacks, one set of underwear, a shirt, and a sweater. I was handed an empty backpack, a sleeping bag, a tarp, and a single-blade knife, which I was told would be used as a survival tool. When I asked about lip balm, he just laughed and said, "No can do. You'll eat it." Welcome to camp!

My three-week journey began with the first of many seven-day tasks I was assigned. I was told it was mandatory to write in my journal every day. It didn't matter what I wrote as long as I participated. The next rule they laid on me was no cursing. I thought, Shit. I had already broken that rule several times since my arrival. I was determined not to let the camp counselors break me, so I kept on using whatever words I wanted.

I rejected every task assigned from the start with a naïve and arrogant "screw you" attitude. It didn't take long for me to realize that my approach wasn't getting me anywhere. After a few days in the woods, I also realized that my perfect escape plan was a total bust. I was stuck. I had no choice but to go with the flow because I was fed up with being the miserable kid. I figured I might as well make the most of my situation because it appeared I was in it for the long haul. Overnight, I went from being the last kid in line to the leader in all of our activities. I was always out in front of the group during our daily long hikes and the first one up the hill. I began to open up a bit, talking to our counselors and asking them about their lives—where they came from and why they were dealing with kids like me.

All of our training during those few weeks led up to the last assignment—being entirely alone for seventy-two hours. We were each handed some paltry food rations that included a single can of soup, one apple, and a canteen of water.

Part of our assignment was to write a letter to our parents, girlfriend, and anyone else we wanted to make peace with before going home. I wrote only my mom and dad to thank them for sending me to this crazy camp. I apologized for all the things I'd done. I was sincere when I wrote their letters. I felt different—more mature and grounded. For the first time in my young life, I had some hope of turning things around for myself.

On the last day, the counselors explained we would make our final one-mile run to an area where all the parents would be waiting for us. It was supposed to be a joyous and momentous occasion of celebration and renewal. Everyone took off running, but my legs felt unexpectedly heavy. I could barely muster the energy for a slow walk. I remember thinking, I don't care if I see my parents. In that three-week period, it was as if I had stepped out of being a child and had become a man. As I edged closer to the finish line, I saw only my mother standing there. Dad was nowhere in sight. When I came up to her, I felt numb and completely unemotional. I realized nothing had changed. I wasn't less angry, and I knew things were going to be worse than ever when I got home.

I found it challenging to get back into my daily life. I became totally detached from everyone and everything around me. I began questioning everything. My life wasn't any better than before I left for Idaho, but I knew I had the inner strength to survive whatever came my way because I had made it through those three hellacious weeks of camp.

When I started ninth grade that fall, it was in a progressive and expensive private school that my mother hoped would challenge me because none of my previous schools had. My new school had small classes and bright kids. On my first day I befriended a guy named Jeff, who was a senior. Like me, he was a crazy punk, so I thought he seemed cool.

"Do you drink beer?" he asked.

"Hell, yeah," I said with just a little too much enthusiasm.

"Meet me in the quad and we'll get hammered."

I was stoked. I loved this school already! By fifth period I was completely wasted. Unfortunately, my mom received that all-too-familiar call. When she came to get me, she said she was spending an enormous amount of money to send me to this school and I was doing worse than ever. Yet despite my adolescent behavior, this was the first school I really liked. I did everything I could to convince her to let me stay. I promised to do better, not party as much, and become responsible. Somehow, even though I had never given her any reason to believe me, she bought my story. I spent the next couple of years pulling A's and B's, but I was still going down the wrong path by using drugs and alcohol.

I was totally out of control. I was stealing and lying, and I didn't care about anyone except my girlfriend and her father's cool car—my dream car—a 1965 Mustang. One night she and I decided to take it out for a spin, and we crashed it. Her parents didn't want me around after that, saying I was a bad influence on their daughter. My mom was reaching her breaking point too.

One day I came home from school to discover that my bedroom

door had been taken off its hinges. That was the final straw for me to pack up my things and leave home. I lived with my buddy Kurt for a while, until Kurt's parents asked me to leave. I ended up sleeping in a friend's van, and I woke up in some pretty strange places more times than I should have. I remember an especially low moment when I awoke hungover and miserable and unable to remember a single thing about the night before. Everything had turned from bad to worse.

Around this time a good friend died from an overdose of heroin. I realized that maybe this whole drug lifestyle wasn't for me. That was one of my first aha moments—a revelation comes during times of pain or adversity, a moment of knowing that enough is enough.

I was now in the eleventh grade and had nowhere to go. I was tired of hanging out with fifty-year-old bikers who were dealing drugs as though they were still young thugs. I knew my father had no patience or tolerance for that lifestyle. One trait I inherited from him was to do everything big in life. If I was doing drugs, I was really doing drugs. If I was getting into trouble, it was really big trouble. If I was in a relationship, I would win you over with all of my heart and soul. That was my whole world, my entire way of being.

In a moment of weakness, I decided to call my dad to reach out for help.

By this time, Dad had built his business into a multimillion-dollar empire. He went from selling Earl Nightingale's *The Strangest Secret* tapes to creating his own platform, speaking to audiences around the country and selling his own how-to tapes, teaching real estate agents how to list and sell properties. He was traveling six days a week, leaving on Sunday and getting back home on Friday. His week was spent speaking in different cities: Monday in Minneapolis, Tuesday in Tampa, Wednesday in New York, Thursday in Chicago, and Friday in Fresno. He was now married to a woman who helped him build their business from the ground up. I hadn't realized how successful he had become because we hadn't spoken for so long.

"Hey, Pops," I said on the phone.

"I'm not your pop" was his response. "You can call me Dad or Mike."

So, this is how it was going to be. I told Dad I had left Mom's house. He was aware I had moved out but didn't seem all that concerned about where I was living or how I was getting by. I asked if I could come live with him.

"I don't have any interest in that, Tom, if you're going to keep living the way you were at your mom's."

I tried to convince him that I was ready for a change. I walked down the hallway of my buddy's house, pulling the long cord behind me so no one would hear as I confessed that I didn't know what I was doing with my life. I told my father I needed some grounding and wanted to have boundaries. I must have said all of the right things because he agreed to come get me.

Dad pulled up in a brand-new red Mercedes 380 SL. I knew Dad was ambitious, but I had no idea he was making that kind of money. He drove me to his home near the ocean in Newport Beach, California. I was mesmerized by the view from his yard. Later that day, he took me to see his office. That was where I got my first taste of what would eventually become the "family" business.

I was fascinated by the whole setup. My universe opened up to the likes of Zig Ziglar, Brian Tracy, and Earl Nightingale. My father was right up there with these guys, making millions of dollars selling and inspiring others to make more money in their business.

Not long after I moved in with Dad, I was kicked out of high school . . . again. Since my father had given me fair warning about my behavior, I wasn't surprised when he immediately told me to get out of his house. I spent the rest of the school year sleeping on the beach or at friends' houses until I finally moved in with my older brother, Matthew, and his fiancée.

I had been working at a local supermarket bagging groceries, so I was comfortable splitting the rent three ways. I worked the midnight-to-9 a.m. shift forty to fifty hours a week, getting in as many hours as possible because no one else wanted that shift. I also started taking continuing education classes so I could get my high school diploma. I had never made it back into the regular classroom. The general equivalency diploma (GED) program required one hour of my time a week. I had my new girlfriend do most of my homework. All I had to do was show up in class, turn in my homework, and get my next assignment.

I remember having an epiphany one night at work after a conversation with my boss, who was twenty years older than I was, doing the same work, and making about the same amount of money. I remember thinking, Is this going to be me twenty years from now?

I had an awful feeling of discontent when I left work that morning. I wondered if stocking and bagging groceries was all I was destined to do.

Was this as good as my life was going to get?

Would I still be living in the same apartment, struggling to get by, and dealing with my same issues? Even though I lived in the worst part of Costa Mesa, the grocery store where I worked was in a fancy part of Corona del Mar. I was surrounded by success and wealth on a daily basis. I realized that great opportunities were available; I just didn't know how I would ever be able to take advantage of them. It was a low moment for me because I didn't see a future that was any better than how I was currently living. That scared the hell out of me.

The next night, I noticed a familiar face coming up one of the aisles of the store. It was my dad. He was wearing a beautifully tailored suit and nice shoes, and he walked with an air of distinction. I was sporting feathered purple hair and was stocking the empty shelves with canned goods. All I could think was, I want to be as successful as he is. One thing was for sure. It certainly wasn't going to happen working at the grocery store.

I didn't stop to say hello. There was no warm hug or reunion. I merely turned to Dad and said, "I know what I want to do with the rest of my life." My father looked surprised but curious. I'm not sure he recognized me at first. And then I said, "I want to run your company."

"Call me when the drugs wear off, Tom." He turned and walked away. That was it. I stood there, momentarily stunned by his cold candor.

I decided to quit my job the next day. I went back to my apartment and began to map out my plan. It had been more than a year since I left my mom's house. Prior to seeing my dad in the grocery store, I hadn't spoken to either of my parents for months. My older brother was still living the life of a rock star—something that had lost its appeal for me.

I got a haircut, dyed my hair back to a neutral brown, and took out my best black clothes. I didn't own a suit, so I did what I could with what I had. I went straight to my dad's house and told him I had my plan all figured out. I explained that what I was doing now was not where I wanted to be. It was the first adult conversation I can recall ever having with Dad.

"I'm so glad you're finally old enough that we can have a relationship, Tom." It had never occurred to me before that moment that my dad, whom I now started referring to solely as Mike or by his initials, MF, wasn't able to relate to me as a kid. He could only talk to me like a colleague. He told me all about his business, from the inside out. He said I would have to learn it from the ground up. I was willing to do whatever it took so I could show him I was being sincere.

I went home and wrote a five-year plan, which culminated with me becoming president of the company. I went back the next day to show Mike my ideas.

"You're hired. Let's go for it." He offered me a salary that was about half of what I had been making at the grocery store, but I didn't care. I was excited to start the next phase of my life, and at eighteen years old, to be working side by side with MF.

LIFE! BY DESIGN

CHAPTER

1

CREATING MY FUTURE

I was excited to be learning the family business. I eagerly began study-ing great motivational experts to learn their secrets and sharpen my skills to become the best leader I could be. I read every book I could get my hands on by authors including Zig Ziglar, Tony Robbins, Wayne Dyer, Brian Tracy, and Kenrick Cleveland. When I was grow-ing up, many of these icons spent time at my dad's house or they shared the same stage. Of course, I had no idea who they were back then. But once I went to work for MF, I recognized the rare opportu-nity I had been given to be exposed to these brilliant minds at such a young age.

I began attending seminars so I could get some face-to-face time with these respected authorities. A couple of years after I started working for MF, I attended a Brian Tracy seminar in Del Mar, Cali-fornia, that changed the course of my life. I was twenty years old. At the time I was making a little over a hundred thousand dollars a year selling my dad's seminars—pretty good for a former drug addict who barely graduated high school. By this time, I was one of Brian's protégés. I had many positive experiences listening to his material and applying his ideas to my daily life. I remember that Brian asked me to stand up in front of the audience that particular day, although I didn't know why.

He introduced me and said, "Here's a kid who is twenty years old, making a pretty good living, and he's one of my best students. He's doing all the right things, except there's one thing missing for Tom to take himself to the next level."

I was stunned. I felt pretty good about where I was and the path I was on. I had no idea what Brian was talking about. I held my breath as he continued.

"Tom needs to get married," Brian announced to the entire room.

I stood there thinking, I'm not even twenty-one yet! I'd had a fake ID in my wallet since I was seventeen years old. I felt I was just coming into my own. I wasn't looking to get married anytime soon, but I was curious. Since I already had Brian's attention, I began firing off questions as fast as I could think them up.

"How do I find the perfect wife?" I asked.

"Go back to your hotel room and write out everything you're looking for in the perfect spouse. Put today's date at the top of that list. I promise you, she'll show up before you can say the word 'Wedding.'"

I had studied with Brian long enough to know that if he tells me to do something, it will have the desired result. With my then girlfriend in tow, and as awkward as it seemed, I went back to my hotel room and did exactly as he asked. I wrote the date, July 17, 1991, at the top of the page and began listing my dream girl qualifications. When I was finished, I folded the page and slipped it into my wallet.

Although I couldn't know it at the time, I'd meet Kathy, my future wife, just thirty days later. Our company was in the middle of marketing a big event that was coming up. One afternoon my phone rang and an enthusiastic woman asked if there was still room for her and five of her friends to attend. I was a young, aggressive, straight-commission salesperson, so this was music to my ears. After we chatted for a few minutes, she said she'd rally her friends and get back to me in a couple of days. I spent the next several weeks attempting to follow up with her, but never spoke to her again. I actually typed the word "flake" next to her name in my computer.

On the day of the event, unbeknownst to me, she showed up with her posse but paid at the door, which meant there would be no commission for me. I was at a private cocktail party for our best clients when I noticed a beautiful woman walk into the room with one of these clients. I was immediately drawn to her. I thought she was stunning. Since we had never met, I walked over and introduced myself. When I looked at her name badge, I went from a would-be Casanova to a hurt schoolboy.

"You're a flake! You never called me, and now you're here?" I asked half serious and half joking.

Kathy and I spoke for a few minutes before I took a chance and asked her out for a drink. Thankfully, she said yes. We spent the rest of the evening talking, connecting, and getting to know each other. There was an instant and electric bond unlike anything I had ever experienced with a woman.

At the seminar the next day, MF acknowledged me from the stage, thanking me for the number of people I helped get to the event and doling out accolades for all of my hard work. I was sitting in the back of the room with Kathy when he said, ". . . all of this the day before his twenty-first birthday!"

I cringed because I knew that Kathy had no idea I was so young. Truth be told, I wasn't your average twenty-year-old kid. I was mature, successful, settled, and experienced. Besides, I didn't like the girls my age. They were too immature for where I was in my life. I wanted to be with a woman who matched or surpassed me emotionally and intellectually. Like my dad, I had tremendous drive and ambition, but I also wanted to build a family.

After Kathy heard how young I was, it took a lot of convincing to get her to go out with me again, but eventually she gave in. I knew I had to make that date count, so I took her to a swanky restaurant in Newport Beach. Once again, the time we spent together was fantastic. When we got into the car after dinner, I could tell that something was on her mind, but she wouldn't tell me what she was thinking. I decided it was best not to push her.

Even though we continued to date, I noticed when we were together that Kathy would introduce me to many of her girlfriends. I was trying to court Kathy, and she was doing everything she could to pass me off. We'd make plans that I thought were dates, and then Kathy would have two or three of her friends meet us. It took me a while to figure out what she was doing, but when I finally did, I told Kathy that I wasn't interested in any of those girls—I was interested only in her.

"Give me a call when you're serious about me because I already know that you're the one I want to marry," I said.

And she was. Kathy epitomized the girl I described on that piece of paper in the hotel room. She had every trait I was looking for and some I hadn't thought of when making my list.

It was close to a year before we met up with each other again. It took that long for Kathy to figure out what *she* wanted.

One night Kathy and I had an argument over something silly. I can't even recall what it was. What I do remember, however, is bringing her the note I wrote to myself on July 17, 1991, that described, in great detail, the woman who would someday become my wife.

At the top I had written, "This is the perfect girlfriend who will walk into my life and we will be perfect together."

1. Brown hair.
2. Blue-green eyes.
3. Extremely understanding.
4. Big personality.
5. Loving but not overpowering.
6. Can make me laugh and loves to laugh.
7. Great family values.
8. Healthy body, healthy mind.
9. Intelligent and the desire to continue to grow.
10. Won't take me for granted.
11. Athletic and competitive.
12. Has a good income and understands money.

Kathy laughed and said, "That's me." But then she said she didn't believe I wrote this list before we actually met. She was convinced I had concocted it as some kind of prop.

I pointed out the date of the note, which was a full month prior to our meeting.

"I loved you when I wrote this list, I loved you the day we met, I loved you when you tried to fix me up with all of your friends, and I love you now and forever."

Kathy didn't buy a word I said. She broke up with me the next day because she thought I was lying to her. She really believed there was no way I could have written such a perfect description of her without first knowing her.

It took a lot of effort to convince Kathy I hadn't made up the story. Fourteen months after we met, Kathy finally agreed to become my wife. She was already my best friend. I wanted to spend the rest of my life with her, build our dream together, and live happily ever after.

Aristotle said the formula for happiness and success is to "First, have a definite, clear, practical ideal; a goal, an objective. Second, have the necessary means to achieve your ends; wisdom, money, materials, and methods. Third, adjust all your means to that end." Brian Tracy put the idea into my head that I could achieve anything I wanted as long as I knew what I was looking for, whether my perfect spouse, the perfect job, weight loss, or any other goal I might have.

All success is predicated on finding what you are passionate about and then relentlessly pursuing every possibility to achieve your dreams. Finding the perfect mate and getting married perhaps were no exceptions.

I worked at my dad's company for fifteen years. I became president nine years after he hired me. I learned the business by doing every job in the organization, from answering phones, sweeping floors, and working in accounting and shipping and receiving, to booking seminars, sales, marketing, coaching, and speaking. My brother Matthew joined the company and together we helped build it from an $8 million-a-year entity to a $36-million-a-year family business.

The first year of my tenure as president was nothing more than a change in the title on my business card. I had a strange and beautiful sensation of achieving something I wanted so much, yet I felt terribly empty after getting it. It was then that I realized that success is not about getting what you want, but who you become along the way.

I didn't achieve my goal of running the company within five years of being hired because I wasn't ready to be an effective leader. I didn't see that as a failure so much as I did fine-tuning who I was in the process of taking on that role.

With all of my entrepreneurial spirit, drive, and determination, I realized that I had become like MF. I spent all of my time away from home, away from my wife and our two sons. I had sworn I wouldn't repeat the same mistakes my father made, and yet there I was walking proudly in his shoes on the same path he had carved out. I gave so much of my life to help build the business, but I wasn't happy.

This is when I began to take a good look at my life.

Was this what I really wanted?

Was I being fair to my family?

To be clear, I wasn't feeling stuck so much as restless. I had a good life. I was earning seven figures, owned two homes, and had a beautiful wife, two amazing kids, and everything I thought I ever wanted.

So why was I feeling so dissatisfied?

Why was I growing fidgety and questioning my identity?

If I took away all of the material things that defined who I was, who would I really be?

For the first time since I was a teenager, I was really confused. I didn't have the answer, and as uncomfortable as that was for me, I had to be okay with it.

I kept hearing about one of MF's mentors, Mike Vance, who had worked with great leaders in business, from Steve Jobs to Jack Welch. The more I learned about him, the more I respected him. I had seen him speak a few times and fell in love with his message about creativity and thinking outside the box. I eventually connected with Mike and asked him if he would coach me in my business. I needed some outside counsel to ask me the tough questions I had been asking my clients and team members for years. I needed a coach. Mike agreed to take me on and immediately got me thinking about my life's purpose and how I wanted to come across to others.

I began fantasizing about creating companies that helped people take on the challenges of life and become responsible for their destiny. None of that had a thing to do with how much money I was making. It had everything to do with quality of life, something I was missing in my own.

I will never forget the *five* huge questions Mike posed to me when I was thinking of making a change.

Why are you here and what's your purpose?
How do you want to come across to others; what are your values?
What are your God-given talents?
Five years from now, how will the world experience you?
Who would you be if you were already there?

None of these questions was easy to answer, but they all got me thinking—hard. It was as if a door had been opened that I never even knew existed. I remember turning to Mike that day and asking him a sixth important question:

"What do I need to let go of so I can take the next step?" This question would become one of the most important tools in defining my future.

Working with Mike was the start of living a life that I would eventually coin "By Design." Mike and I spent weeks mapping out my future, which required answering every one of his five questions in great detail. It took a lot of time, thought, and soul-searching to get to the core of each question. I wanted to be as authentic and honest as I could because there was so much riding on my answers.

Looking back, that coaching session and the weeks that followed pointed me toward wanting to leave my father's company. The relationship with MF had become strained over the years. It was clear that, professionally speaking, we had come to the end of the road because I was moving in one direction while Dad continued to move in another. When I was named president, MF essentially retired and was rarely seen at the office, but he still wanted a hand in the day-to-day operations of the business.

Four years after he left, MF called to say he wanted to come back to work. There was no doubt in my mind that if he came back to the company, he would end up running it, which meant I would be pushed out.

I went home that night and talked it over with my wife. I told her that if he came back to work, I would have to leave. Quitting isn't part of who I am—not then or now. She suggested I take some time to think it over before making any final decisions.

I began rationalizing my choice to resign. I told myself I didn't need to run the company anymore. I thought I could easily shift my energy and attention toward some of the other ventures I had started but hadn't been able to give enough time or attention in order to make them successful.

A few weeks later, I sat down with MF to explain how I felt. I told him that I had decided to step down as president but would continue coaching and wanted to remain his partner in all of the other businesses we shared. He said that didn't work for him. He told me to take more time off to think it over. He acknowledged that I had worked hard to get the business to its peak level but didn't think I was seeing things as clearly as he was. Christmas and New Year's were just around the corner, so we decided to reconvene after the holidays.

I didn't need extra time to make up my mind, although I didn't officially step down until January 2003. Shortly after that, I announced to my team that even though we had had a great run together, it was clear I had taken them as far as I could. I explained that MF would take over the daily running of the company, but I would still be there and always available if they needed me.

Toward the end of 2003, I concluded that I'd been riding this train far too long. It was impossible for it to go in opposite directions without breaking apart. I didn't have the stamina to find joy in my work. If I walked away, I'd be leaving behind MF—who despite everything was my best friend, my business partner, and my mentor—along with all of my siblings, who were now each a part of the company too.

Leaving would be as complicated as a divorce. We had assets together and emotional ties that would be severed. I had worked fifteen years supporting someone else's vision. It was time to start living my own. The only solution I had was to quit. But in MF's world, there is no leaving and staying in good graces. Several times in the past I had tried to talk to him about how I was feeling, but he never wanted to hear what I had to say.

It all finally came to a head toward the end of the year on a flight home from an event in Miami. I was tired of coaching for MF; I no longer wanted to speak for him and I didn't want to continue running the other companies we were involved in together. I looked MF in the eyes and told him, "I can't do this anymore. I love you and the family, but I've got to follow my heart and do my own thing." MF's response was to "go on vacation. You're just burned out and tired. You'll get over it." He was still refusing to hear what I was saying. I spent the rest of the flight fighting back my tears. I didn't want him to see how upset I was. The next few hours were awkward for both of us. By the time we flew over Las Vegas, I had gone through all the emotion and drama in my mind. When we landed, I got into a waiting car without ever saying goodbye or looking back.

I put together my letter of resignation that night and handed it in a few days later. In the letter, I thanked MF for all he had done for me—for all he had taught me along the way and the opportunities he had extended. I wrote how much I wished he and I could have some level of joy in our relationship. I had spent years trying to get MF to love and respect me—something I wanted more than anything. But I knew the time had come for me to step away and let him run his company as he saw fit.

A few days later, I received it back in the mail with one word written across the top: "Unacceptable." MF didn't realize I wasn't asking his permission to leave. He avoided me for the next thirty days. When I finally called and was able to tell him I was really through, I explained that the whole situation had become toxic and unbearable, that all the money in the world wouldn't bring me back because it wasn't about money, that I wasn't sure what I was going to do, but we could work out the details later.

The first week in December, we announced my resignation to the company. I began to make thirty-six of the most difficult coaching calls I had ever made. One at a time, I told my clients and dear friends that I was leaving the organization. After the first few calls, I realized this approach wouldn't work because every client wanted to know where I was going and what time we would talk again next week. At my lunch break, I phoned MF and told him he would have to call the rest of the clients because they didn't have any interest in another coach; they wanted to continue to work with me. I wanted MF to make it clear to the rest of my clients that continuing a relationship with me wasn't an option. Frustrated, he slammed down the phone and made the calls. They were short and to the point. From what I was told, they went something like this:

"Hello, Bob? This is Mike Ferry. I'm calling to tell you that Tom is leaving the company, but I've selected the perfect coach for you to take his place. His name is John and he will be in touch. Goodbye."

After he and I hung up the phone, I closed my files, turned off my computer, and realized I was no longer working for the Mike Ferry Organization. I was now free.

Shortly after I left the office that last day, my cellphone began ringing off the hook. I wasn't ready to deal with the fallout that soon, so I let all of the calls go to my voice mail for the rest of the day. Six clients left me similar messages saying they wanted to be my first client. That was hard to ignore because six people would be enough business to get me up and running. My wife and I decided we had to honor the wishes of the people I had built up a relationship with, but I didn't want to pilfer clients from MF. It didn't feel right. So we decided to start a small business that we would run from our home. I called my mentor and good friend Bill Mitchell to ask his opinion. He summed things up, as only Bill could:

"Your dad's business is going one direction and you are moving in another." He told me I could go after an entirely different market than MF's without jeopardizing my integrity.

I could live with that.

I decided to focus on high-end Realtors, a market that MF had never gained any serious traction in and that basically he didn't work in. Shortly after leaving his company, I began marketing my services to the biggest and best Realtors in the business. There were 270,000 real estate brokers between Santa Barbara and San Diego, so I bootstrapped it up, went out there and began to sell my services and build my new company.

I turned away 350 of MF's clients who came to me within the first year after I left his company. I decided that taking them on as clients wasn't worth the money or the headache that surely would have come with having to fight against MF. I took the high road every step of the way.

. . .

I finished my first year in business with $2.19 million in revenue. In my first two years of business, I went from nonexistent to the third largest company in the real estate success coaching industry.

Seven years later, my company is thriving. I have expanded my services to include professionals beyond real estate. Today I personally coach CEOs of companies, the Hollywood elite, and other entrepreneurs. Other coaches in my firm are working with everyone from CEOs of start-up ventures to CEOs of the home. We work with schoolteachers and sales executives, everyday people just like you who are interested in shifting their lives from by default to By Design.

The goal of this book is to help you find balance and create purpose and passion in *your* life. Throughout our journey together, I will ask you the same challenging questions Mike asked of me, which helped me make one of the most difficult yet freeing decisions of my life and career. And if that isn't enough to get you thinking, I will continue to push you to ask yourself several other questions designed to help you get a clear picture of what your life is like from the outside looking in. Your answers to those questions will dictate the outcome of your success toward my goal of teaching you to live By Design.

I created my six-step plan to help you not only discover what's not working in your life, but also how you can shift from living by default to By Design by creating purpose and passion in your life. Each of these steps will require you to dig deep and face your weaknesses, fears, and flaws. Let me be perfectly candid. *We all have these.* I will say this again. We *all* suffer from emotional damage from our past and the negative things we tell ourselves about our weaknesses, fears, and flaws. We *all* get caught up in daily dramas and suffer extensively from our attachment to the opinions of others. The good news is we don't have to. If we can adapt, learn, and grow by letting go of these attachments, living By Design will become a much less daunting and more achievable task. So, how do you learn to do this?

Read on.

My company motto is *Strategy Matters and Passion Rules!*

Why?

In today's world, it takes the right strategies to live By Design. These strategies are the six steps outlined in this book.

Passion is the power source that drives us and makes us persist over time and in the face of adversity. And to have passion you have to love what you do. Passion is a necessary component of success, but alone it is not enough. Vision without action deteriorates into daydreaming. Without persistence, passion fades.

I'm not a guru. I am a regular guy whose life's mission is to make a difference in other people's lives. I have been exposed to more, and perhaps different, models of excellence than you have. These models have helped me develop and brand my own model of excellence, a model you can now benefit from and experience for yourself.

I am one of the fortunate guys in this world who wakes up every day eager, excited, fired up, and ready to get to work. I love my wife and two sons. Against many obstacles, I have created an extraordinary life. Am I somehow luckier than you?

No.

I simply choose to live my life By Design—not by default.

Are you ready to get started?

Then let's go!

Congratulations . . . You have made it through Chapter 1. Now go to my website www.TomFerry.com/resources to view "Life by Design," a video from me to you!

—Tom

PHASE

I

LIVING BY DEFAULT

BY DEFAULT VERSUS BY DESIGN

Have you ever played the lottery? Who hasn't bought a ticket with the hope that those six numbers will hit, and bam! your life will instantly change? All of your troubles would go away if you had millions of dollars in the bank, right? Wrong! You'd still have the same issues, only with a much bigger balance in your checkbook.

Everybody already knows, of course, that money doesn't buy happiness. Despite the enormous financial success that several of my clients had achieved, their lives were a mess before we began working together. You see, happiness and success aren't about how much money you have in the bank but how well you are living your life. I don't mean how grandly or extravagantly you're living but rather the quality of life you're living.

To fully understand what holds us back from living to our fullest potential, we have to do two important things. First, we have to recognize that most people live life *by default.* What I mean by this is they fail to decide, or stop deciding, how they want their lives to be, or they are unwilling to do *whatever* it takes to live to their fullest potential. Or worse, they simply accept things as they are and believe they have no say in the result. But the bottom line about living by default, in my view, is that it represents *choosing to be a victim*!

Let me say that again: If we're not leading our fullest life, if we feel ourselves constrained or victimized by outside circumstances, it is because, in essence, we have accepted that this is our lot, and we have made the choice to live a life of diminished expectations, to accept our lives and circumstances as they are. We sit around saying things like:

"It's the economy."

"When will the government [or my boss, my spouse, my kids] do something about this?"

"I don't have enough money to live the way I used to or want to."

"It's always been this way."

"I'm too old for change."

"I feel like I can't compete with the younger kids coming in to do the same job."

And the granddaddy of them all (I say this because we've all said something like this at one time or another): "I have to wait for _____ before I can make a change."

Does any of this sound familiar?

Does it remind you of anyone in particular?

These are the hallmarks of someone living by default, someone who's accepted those "reasons" as valid and legitimate instead of seeing them for what they are—plain old-fashioned excuses.

Why is it that some people live their lives full of love, abundance, and purpose—what I would call rich and full lives—while others live in a state of fear, lack, and indecision? It is because most people see themselves as victims. They're always suffering. In tough economic times, adversity is destined to be on your path. Are you worried about losing your job, home, marriage, health, or money? The question isn't how did you get here, but what will you do now?

When you realize that you've been living your life by default, you will become aware that you are responsible for your choices. With twenty years and nearly thirty thousand hours of success coaching behind me, I have learned that most people are comfortable suffering and too quickly accept things as they are rather than choosing to change or try something new.

Do you know someone like this?

Can you relate to this person?

Perhaps it's you.

A small percentage of people are happy, successful, and healthy and don't let the bumps in life get them down.

Do you think they were born that way or did they *learn* to live that way?

Did they get there by default or was it By Design?

The people living By Design live by a different set of rules. They know an upset is just an upset, their problems are assets, and the past is where it belongs—somewhere behind them. They aren't victims; they're victors, heroes if you will, because they are willing to jump through hoops to live the life they dream of. I've met extremely successful businesspeople as well as people who don't have two nickels to rub together who fall into this category. Living By Design isn't about how much money you have. It's a frame of mind that positively impacts every core area of your life. Living By Design isn't easy, but it is hugely rewarding, and that, my friend, is our goal.

Do you really want to be healthy, happy, feel more in control, inspired, and be in a loving relationship? Or are you okay being one of the 123 million Americans who are unhappy and discontented with their lives? I have been to the lowest point in my life—waking up in the gutter, wasted on drugs with no hope of ever changing my life. If I can turn my life around, so can you.

Now, I didn't do it alone and I didn't jump in blind. I had guides, mentors, teachers, coaches, and a plan that helped me choose wisely and get on the right path.

Everyone needs a helping hand from time to time, someone to reach out and say, I'm here for you. That's why I have written this book. Whether you're in the depths of despair or simply stuck on a plateau, just living a good life, I am that reached-out hand, ready, willing, and able to help you live an extraordinary life. Why? Because I believe you deserve it. The bigger question is, do you?

My job as a success coach is to talk to clients from a business perspective about every last detail in their lives. I get paid to produce a specific result, so I can't view just one aspect of my clients. I have to see all the parts that make up the whole of who they are. I know that if their personal life is in shambles, no matter what I suggest, their business life won't get any better until those issues are worked out. Their business might slightly improve, but it will never experience that quantum leap my clients are seeking and expecting when we work together. That makes me life coach, business coach, therapist, best friend, and sometimes father, brother, and devil's advocate. Above all, they know I have their back and will do whatever it takes to make them successful.

Check this out. I repeat several key points throughout this book. This is intentional and meant to drive home each message. I find the more times I say the right thing over and over again, the less likely you are to forget it. So, if you're ready for a life change, to find your passion and to live at an extraordinary level, this is your wake-up call. No more pity parties. No more excuses. No more procrastination.

Are you ready?

Turn the page.

WAKE UP!

Three years after I started my own company, I was on a family vacation in Mexico when I had one of the most inspiring "dad" moments of my life. It also turned out to be one of the most poignant wake-up calls I've ever had. I was in the ocean teaching my then seven-year-old son, Michael, how to surf. We were on a small break off the sandy shore of the hotel where we were staying, a perfect spot to get Michael up on a board. Three hours after we hit the surf, I noticed Kathy, my wife, on the beach packing up our things to head back to the hotel. I turned to Michael and said, "Time to head in, dude."

"Just one more wave, Daddy. Please, can we stay for one more?"

It was official. My son was hooked on surfing. I loved it. I told him I was going to ride the next big wave in and he could stay in the water to catch one more for himself. I began paddling toward the shore when I noticed the perfect wave about to break. I jumped up on my board, looked to my right, and saw Michael up on his board directly next to me with a smile as big as the ocean on his face. For the first time ever, we were riding the same wave. It was an absolute moment of joy. There are no words to describe the feelings I had watching my boy cruising next to me. I will never forget what my son and I shared in that moment. Worried he might not be able to maneuver the wave as well with me next to him, I cut out to let him ride the wave on his own. Plus, it gave me the opportunity to watch him ride that last wave all the way in to shore.

I was a few yards back, paddling in until the water was too shallow. I began gingerly walking among the rocks as I made my way toward the white sandy beach. All of a sudden, I hit my leg on something under the water and cut my shin wide open. I didn't think much of it at the time. It stung for a second but I had to keep moving. As I walked up onto the beach, blood was dripping down my leg. I must have cut it on the jagged edge of a rock. My wife and I did what we could to clean it up and stop the bleeding, before making our way back to the hotel with the kids.

When we returned to our home in California a couple of days later, I noticed that the cut on my leg looked badly infected. I went to a local emergency room to have it looked at. The doctor gave me a tetanus shot and said to keep off my feet for the next couple of days. Was he kidding? I am not the kind of guy who takes days off during the week, especially because I was still getting my company up and running. I had just returned from the first vacation I had taken since getting my company off the ground. I had no time or desire to be out of the office for a few days. As hard as it was for me to do, I begrudgingly called my assistant and told her to clear my schedule.

By the time I got home, I began feeling sick. I was having an adverse reaction to the tetanus shot. I climbed into bed, spiked a fever, and before I knew it began slipping in and out of consciousness. A doctor friend assured me that I would be fine but I'd have to ride out the fever until it broke. Thankfully, it did just that around midnight. Although I was feeling a little better, I would now definitely be out of commission for the next couple of days.

I spent the following day taking it easy—something I wasn't used to doing. I watched television for a few minutes, read a magazine, surfed the Net, and lounged around for a couple of hours. But it wasn't restful because I felt that there was something more I could be doing with this found time. I decided to read all of the journals I had kept since I was twenty years old. I read stories of my life over the past sixteen years until I stumbled across the one that had the five fundamental questions that Mike Vance had asked me when I was stuck in my rut before leaving MF's company.

I stared at those five questions and my responses for several minutes as I thought about the impact they had on my life the first time I answered them. I remembered the clarity and strength I had when I realized that the situation I had been in was toxic and not right for my soul, my family, and my destiny. At the time, my entire life had been about supporting someone else's vision and not my own.

As I lay in bed reading the journal, I realized that this was a wake-up call. I didn't know I was looking for greater purpose and meaning until I began asking myself the same five questions again.

I looked at the first question, "Why are you here and what's your purpose?" This time my answer came back quite different than it did before. Prior to leaving MF's company, my answer was all about following my own path, being my own man, breaking away and leaving. It was time to allow my siblings to rise and take the reins of the family business while I broke away and started my own company. Now that I was on my own, I found myself asking, "Is this all there is?" more often than I expected. Of course, the answer to that question was easy—no. What I really wanted to do was inspire millions of people to live and work By Design, to help them wake up from their coma and begin living their best life.

I was getting inspired and fired up as I took myself through this exercise that day. I began typing my answers into my laptop as quickly as my fingers would move. I had a new life vision to map out. I wanted to give people the tools, structure, and accountability to get out from under their fears and live their life By Design, just as I had done.

The next question was "How do you want to come across to others; what are your values?" I already knew I could continue teaching seminars and workshops on the subject. But what I really wanted to do was write a *New York Times*, Amazon, *USA Today*, *Publishers Weekly*, and *Wall Street Journal* bestseller. I wanted that book translated into twenty or more languages so it could have a strong impact on people around the world. I wanted to be on television talking about my By Design lifestyle, meeting people like Oprah and Larry King, and appearing on all of the top talk and newsmagazine shows instilling the words "By Design" into our everyday vernacular.

Was this a lofty goal?

It sure was.

Was I afraid to reach for it?

Absolutely not.

I tell all of my clients that their dreams usually die on the table when they are still in the idea stage. As I was creating my new vision, I saw my ultimate contribution to the planet as being infinitely bigger than what I had been working on. The only way I could grow into that vision was to think bigger and wider than I ever had.

I read the third question—"What are your God-given talents?" I realized now that I was on my own, I was able to speak more freely about what was on my mind and in my heart about strategies that I know work versus being confined to someone else's message. I knew that my God-given talent was that I could wake people up and inspire them to live more By Design.

Question number four, "Five years from now, how will the world experience you?" was easy to answer. I would be a bestselling author and a respected success coach helping people from CEOs to students live an extraordinary life. I could inspire people to get into better shape, or help them change the quality of their life for the better, and everything in between.

I know that By Design living impacts all areas of our lives, so answering Mike's final question—"Who would you be if you were already there?"—would be a piece of cake because I had the vision. Now all I needed to do was build on it. I would have to find and assemble the right team to help me achieve my vision, and then slowly and methodically, By Design, lay out a plan to achieve everything I had imagined.

Several hours had passed as I answered those fundamental questions. By the time I finished typing the last words to my answers, I was exhilarated and filled with joy at the possibilities for my future.

The wound on my leg, the reaction to the tetanus shot, and three days off from work turned out to be a wonderful gift that allowed me to be present with what I really wanted out of life.

When faced with big life questions, most people get stuck because they're afraid to look deep inside themselves and face all of the baggage that holds them back. Instead, they sit around complaining, saying they don't have the time to answer the five questions that could change their lives. Let me tell you something. Living By Design is not about *having* the time. It's about *making* the time—and *your life* a priority.

Answering these questions for a second time helped me identify a bigger vision and future for myself. I didn't even know I needed a change, but those couple of days became the next major turning point in my life.

I could have kept reading those five questions, scanning through them like the rest of the pages in my journals, but I didn't. I used the questions to help me reflect on who I am, where I am, and what I am all about. I dug deep to find the answers that ultimately set me on the course that I am now on, which brought me here to you. If you doubt the power and process of living By Design in any way, the manifestation of that day is in your hands right now. That's right. You are reading my book, the culmination of that vision.

Now that you know two of my biggest life wake-up calls, are you ready to get started on your own? When I take on new clients, I make it clear that I will not hold their hands and tell them that everything will be okay. And you, my reader, are no different. If you want someone to comfort and coddle you through life's challenges, I suggest you talk to your mother, wife, boyfriend, girlfriend, or best friend, or schnauzer, who will tell you whatever you want to hear so you feel better. That is not my role. My job is to help you face the hard truth, get honest, create a vision for your life, to stop living with excuses of why you "can't," and start living with the belief that "Yes, You Can!"

You picked up this book because somewhere along the way you realized you're not satisfied. I doubt you bought this book because your life is already extraordinary but you think it can be even better. Am I right? You know something's up with your relationship, health, finances, mindset, or emotions, but you just don't know what to do to make things better. This book involves a tremendous amount of self-examining, but if you trust the process and participate in the evolution of living By Design, you will find your efforts greatly rewarded.

Think of your life as a giant flowing river. Some people choose to stand on the bank watching the river flow by. These people are so stuck in their lives that they're not even paying attention to the beautiful river. Others spend all their time in the river trying to wade against the current, fighting the natural flow and struggling to stay afloat.

Living life By Design is the opposite of both. It is the acknowledgment that there's a current that you have to go with, but you can either navigate around or learn to remove the occasional boulders that block, change, and disrupt your flow. Or, if for whatever reason you're in the wrong river altogether, you can get out and find another one.

I've got a challenge for you right out of the gate. I am going to ask you to consider a lot of thoughtful questions about what hasn't been working in your life. The questions I will ask are designed to resuscitate you. There is no shot of morphine at the end of this journey to ease the inevitable pain, but there is the promise that if you participate in the process, you will be awake, perhaps for the first time in your life, and well on your way to living your life By Design. Are you up for that?

There's no judgment or "do it my way" philosophy here.

This is *your* life. Let's just have it be By Design.

Okay. Here we go.

As we proceed, know that I honor your bravery and desire to improve the quality of your life. As in Las Vegas, what happens here stays here. It's between you and me. I have your back and will get you through the process. But recognize, as cliché as it may sound, no pressure, no diamond!

So with all of this in mind, let's do a quick check on your personal level of awareness. Listed below are some simple questions. Think of this like the old game show *Password*. Say whatever comes to your mind. Don't edit your responses. Just go with your gut reaction.

> *How do you feel about your career?*
> *How do you feel about your relationships?*
> *How do you feel about your health and stamina?*
> *How do you feel about your income and current financial status?*
> *What areas of your life are you avoiding? (C'mon! Answer the question!)*
> *Is there someone or something in your life you feel incomplete with?*

Where in your life do you feel the most pressure?
What are your consistent issues or struggles?
What bothers you about your current lifestyle?
How do you feel about change?

EXERCISE

Examine the areas of your life where you experience resistance and write them down. If you are stuck, reread the previous questions. They will steer you in the right direction.

Okay. Let's do a quick check. Do your answers make you feel worse or full of promise?

When you look at your situation, can you identify what has been holding you back from living a truly extraordinary life? Some people say it's fear; others simply aren't comfortable with change. Still others aren't aware of what's wrong in the first place, living in denial and not acknowledging that there is always room for improvement.

I don't believe there are stupid people in this world, but I do think there are people who simply don't have an awareness of or have not been exposed to what is possible. They point the finger of blame at everyone or everything around them without acknowledging their feelings or responsibility in the matter.

They say things like:

It's not me, it's "the man."

It's not me, it's the way my parents raised me.

It's not me, it's my team.

It's much easier to play the blame game than it is to accept responsibility for the resistance in our lives. Most people believe that life is supposed to be hard, that change is scary, that conflict and struggle are normal. While all of these things are true, none of them has to consume you. I deal with conflict, I have struggles, I face hardships and challenges, but I don't let them rule me. Challenges don't own or define me. It isn't the way I live my life, and I am happy to say that you don't have to either.

When you get present to the notion that you are responsible for what you create in life, you can then own it, push it aside, and/or make new and better choices. It's all about your awareness and new action. I want to help you get to a place where you have clarity and vision to see things as they really are.

In marketing, advertisers know that the average human being is exposed to more than three thousand marketing messages a day. We live in a stimulus response world. Everything around us is stimulus, so although we've become numb to some of it, most stimuli have a way of infiltrating our barriers. Most people become irresponsible in the split second between stimulus and response. That's when our mind reacts to something even before we know what it is. We take that response down a negative path and prepare ourselves for doom and gloom.

For example, in a relationship, there are four words that generally provoke a worst-case-scenario response: "We need to talk."

Uh-oh.

You're getting dumped, or are about to hear a confession of infidelity, or your partner has feelings for someone else. Whatever it is, those words conjure up negative thoughts, right?

Your unconscious mind is where all of the data files of your life experiences are stored and where you naturally go to find your response when a stimulus occurs. Scientists believe that every social act is a response to a preceding act of another individual or event. A stimulus response can be a rise in emotions and passions and can also cause a physical reaction. For example, a physical stimulus response is feeling the pain and burning of placing your hand on a hot stove and pulling it away. An emotional stimulus response might be reacting to a new lover because of something a former lover did. It's crying when you see a sad movie, or feeling butterflies in your stomach when you think about someone you are crazy in love with.

Think about a song that, every time you hear it, transports you back in time to a place, event, or person it reminds you of. Even a particular scent can bring you back in time. This is all part of how our senses anchor us to the past. Almost every reaction or action in our lives is a product of conditioning, experience, exposure, and the environment.

Becoming aware of these responses will help remove the self-induced struggle you face. It will help you understand that life is a continuous cycle of learning and growing and then understanding what you need to do so you can get better results in every area of your life.

Sounds easy, right? But it's not, because most people are living in what I refer to as an *active coma*. They're alive and functioning but appear to be plugged into an imaginary life support, hoping that someday when they wake up everything will be okay. Think about it: They've become victims of world circumstances and they're doing little to nothing about it! They're suffering with a poor economy, housing crises, politics, their finances or lack thereof, their relationships, their health, and their emotional well-being, just to name a few. And they're stuck, concerned, worried, and afraid to break out from their comfort zone to take action. They're afraid to change, afraid to try something new or try a new approach; they're in a coma.

You're living in a coma if you wake up at the same time every morning, read the newspaper, have breakfast, kiss someone goodbye (or not), get into the car or hop onto the bus or train, listen to the same thing on the radio or your iPod, take the same route every day, wear almost the same outfit you wore the day before, show up at the office, and do the same old routine over and over until it's time to go home, where it might be meatloaf Monday or taco Tuesday. There's no creativity in that kind of life and no expression of joy.

It's important to note that while I am all about routines and habits, I am focused on those that bring you power and joy and move you one step closer to your goals and dreams.

I had a client who was in complete denial about her children's obnoxious behavior. She told me that her family traveled with friends—but only once, because no one wanted to travel with them again after that. After her kids came home from play dates, other parents called to say that her child did this or that and made the other children cry. She took no responsibility for her kids' behavior. She wouldn't address the issues and couldn't understand why everyone reacted so negatively to her children. Her husband was not aware of the problems either because he spent more time in front of the television or his computer than he did in the bedroom with his wife or spending quality time with his kids. And although my client was completely aware of her husband's absence in their lives, still she said nothing to him. This is a classic example of a woman who is living in a coma. She doesn't see things as they are. She doesn't address reality. She doesn't react to anything going on around her. She's not doing anything wrong, her kids are perfect, and her husband is always there for her. Everything is "fantastic," but her whole world is a lie.

Do you know anyone like this?

I used to coach a man, let's call him Donald, who was consumed with his number one competitor in business because that company was consistently outperforming Donald's. It was growing and thriving while Donald's was shrinking and becoming irrelevant in the marketplace. Donald spent all of his time writing memos and reports to anyone who would listen, proclaiming that his competitor was wrong about the future, instead of focusing on changing his own business model and services to remain a player in the game. Donald was living in a coma. His strategy hadn't changed in years even though his clients were adapting to new trends and changes in the marketplace. He actually sent out letters saying that his competitor was leading its clients down a path that would *destroy* their businesses if they followed its advice. Donald's ego wouldn't allow him to get out of his own way. Instead of listening to what he had to say, Donald's clients began canceling their contracts and moving their business to his competitor.

The moral of this story is, you either adapt or die. It's one of the simplest rules of business. Failing to address the issues and make the necessary changes is a recipe for disaster. Donald found that out the hard way. The irony here is that instead of changing his approach to accommodate the times, he fired me as his coach, placing me at the top of his blame list for pointing out the obvious. Unfortunately, it's only a matter of time before his business will cease to exist. His stubbornness and failure to acknowledge his own resistance to change will be the reason he'll be forced into an early retirement.

I admit that I had been living in a big coma when I was working for MF. I often think back to those years as my "coma[2]." I knew I had been terribly unhappy and dissatisfied with my position in MF's company, but I kept right on with my daily routine pretending everything was great—accepting mediocrity and leading others to believe that what they saw in me was genuine and sincere. When I told MF how I felt, his suggestion was to get away for a few weeks, think it over, take a breather. What he was really saying to me was "Get over it!"

Martin Luther King once said, "The ultimate measure of a man is not where he stands in moments of comfort and convenience, but where he stands at times of challenge and controversy." So, despite MF's efforts to get me to reconsider, I had made up my mind to resign. Nothing could stop me because I had created a clear vision for what I wanted and where I was headed even if I had no clue how I was going to get there. My decision to leave MF's company woke me from my active coma. For the first time in years, I was awake, aware, and full of hope and fear. The latter, you will find out, can sometimes be a good thing.

You might be reading this and thinking, Well, *I'm* not in a coma. That may be true, but consider that as of July 2008, there were more than 123 million Americans who were either struggling or suffering, partly, but not entirely due to the current economic crisis. As things progressively get worse, that number continues to skyrocket, eclipsing the number of thriving Americans month after month.

These are the same people who are spending billions of dollars on medication to try to feel better. They've flatlined, they're shut down and repressed and avoid the truth, and they are living with this thought: Someday it will get better. They're in an active coma, and it is time for them to wake up.

According to a new Centers for Disease Control (CDC) report, antidepressants are America's most prescribed drugs, more than meds for high blood pressure, high cholesterol, or asthma. The report claims that prescriptions for antidepressants rose 48 percent between 1995 and 2002, and accounted for 118 million of the 2.4 billion drugs prescribed in 2005.

What if I told you I can help these people shift from struggling to thriving in a matter of weeks without using antidepressants to help them feel better about themselves—and before their circumstances spiral so far out of control that they become prisoners of their own lives?

This book is *not* called "Some Aspect of Your Life, If It's Conven-ient and Happens to Miraculously Fall into Place By Design." It's about your *whole* life. We've got to look at the whole picture. And to do that, we need to examine all of the pieces of the puzzle. Let's get started.

CHAPTER

THE PROBLEM OF NO PROBLEMS

As part of our process together, I'm going to hold up a mirror for you. If you don't like what you see, don't break the mirror—take action and change your life.

You may be thinking that your life is peachy, that you're on the right path and don't need to make drastic changes. The likelihood, though, is that if you bought this book, you're looking for help. You may not yet be totally aware of what areas need your attention, but something inside you is saying, "There's got to be more." I refer to that as "the problem of no problems."

It would be easy for me to give my clients answers to their problems. What's hard is to help them understand *why* they have issues in the first place. If you're thirsty, I can give you a bottle of water, but I'd rather you know why you're thirsty and talk about the natural ways to quench your thirst. To do that, we both have to dig deep. And for all of us, that starts with a clear understanding of where you come from, where you're currently living, and where you see yourself in the future.

If you want a vivid picture of what your life looks like to others, ask five people around you to tell you about yourself. Give them permission to be totally, brutally honest. Let them know you came to them for their candor—that you trust them and are ready and willing to hear the truth. Ask these people to tell you about the things you do they admire. What actions do they think are working for you? Then ask what they see that doesn't work or isn't in alignment with what you say you want. (We *all* have these discrepancies!)

A friend recently took this advice and asked five of his closest pals, including me, to tell him something he does that is not working.

All five people told him he stretches the truth—sometimes just to look good personally or professionally.

Whoa. When five people tell you you're basically a liar, it's time to make a change. Once again, the problem of no problems reared its head.

When we expressed what we saw that didn't work, my friend was shocked. He thought that no one knew he stretched the truth. It wasn't so much his fabrications that mattered as it was why he felt he needed to stretch the truth to have us see him in a certain way. He was addicted to the opinions of other people, meaning he cared so much about what other people thought of him that he was willing to lie to gain their approval. (I go much deeper into this subject in the next chapter.) My friend was desperate for everyone to believe that he was more than he actually was. When we delved deeper into his reasons for doing this, what came out was his low self-esteem. When he looked in the mirror, he wasn't happy with what he saw, so he took every chance he got to project what he *wanted* to see in the mirror. I've seen this pattern of false projection many times. Somewhere in their addicted minds, these people believe that if they keep lying about themselves, eventually other people will see it as the truth. Unfortunately, this strategy does not work.

Remember that this man asked five of his closest buddies to tell him the truth about himself, so he was clearly looking for change. When we divulged our observations, his level of awareness went up, which made him a more responsible person. He now knows that if we knew he was stretching the truth, his spouse, co-workers, and everyone else he had a connection with knew it too. That newfound awareness was enough motivation for him to make the choice to change. Today, instead of saying everything is "great" in his life, or everything is "working," he has the power to admit when things aren't going right or he's having an off day—something he'd never have done before this exercise.

EXERCISE

Ask five people around you to tell you about yourself. Ask them to answer the following three questions:

1. What do you admire about me?
2. What do you see that I do that really works for me?
3. What actions do you see that I do that really don't work for me?

Give these five people permission to be totally honest. Ask them to tell you about the things you do they admire and what negative habits you have that everyone else knows but you can't see. Be prepared to hear what they have to say without judging or being defensive. This is the start of looking inside.

Knowing what you know about your past, what do you think is stopping you from doing all of the things you used to dream about as a child, as a young adult, when you started your first job, when you met the love of your life, and everything else you used to think about in that dreamy state?

To answer this question, you also have to decide what you're not taking responsibility for in life.

Stop.

Don't breeze past this. Really think about what I'm asking you to consider. What is it you're not taking responsibility for in your life?

Look, all of us have had conversations in our heads where we've said to ourselves, "I'll deal with this later," "it is what it is," "whatever," and "there's nothing I can do about this—it's out of my control." When we're challenged by something that is painful, emotional, or confronting, our natural tendency is to seek something that will immediately make us feel better. My asking you what you are not taking responsibility for in your life might be all it takes for you to put down this book, click on the TV, and call me an idiot so *you* won't have to confront *your* issues. Am I right?

Oh. You're still reading. Cool.

Let's face it. It doesn't take much to push someone to that place of discomfort. It could be something as simple as trying on a pair of jeans that are too tight, a misunderstood look from your spouse, or one of the questions being posed to you here that potentially sends you into a spiral. How do most people usually react? Instead of confronting their feelings, they choose to avoid the issue by moving on to something else to escape their feelings altogether. Some people will eat, have a few drinks, work out, or lose themselves at the office or in front of the television so they don't have to deal with what's really holding them back. Whatever you do, remember that your reaction is the effect of a much greater issue that you are resisting.

Listen, avoiding issues doesn't make them go away. If you are going to live By Design, you have to confront all areas of who you are. This means challenging your flaws, weaknesses, mistakes, and imperfections. What you and I will do together is bring the awareness of these issues to the surface so you can face them, deal with them, conquer them, and move on.

> When you're feeling pain, angst, or stress, what do you naturally gravitate toward? Do you confront the issue or avoid it?

A few years ago, I presented a seminar that I felt very good about afterward. I thought I crushed it. When I got back to my office a couple of days later, however, I found an email from a woman who had been in attendance that day. The letter started out by complimenting me and the overall message I conveyed. Her note took a downward turn when I read the words "I've got to get this off my chest." The woman explained I had said something she found so offensive that she had to get up and leave thirty minutes early. She is the mother of a child with cerebral palsy. During a Q&A, someone from the audience asked me a ridiculous question, to which I responded, "Don't be retarded." My poor choice of words upset this woman to the point of making her leave. I was stunned when she shared her feelings, because my intention would never be to hurt someone by being careless with something I said. I felt awful and didn't want to read further. I closed the email and tried not to think about it the rest of the afternoon. As much as I tried to push her message from my thoughts, however, I spent the rest of the day accepting the fact that I had been careless with my choice of words. I needed to own my mistake so it wouldn't consume me a moment longer. I picked up the phone and called her. We spoke for twenty minutes, the bulk of which we spent talking about her child and who she has had to be as a mother and businessperson to continually thrive under these conditions.

When we hung up, surprisingly I still didn't feel complete about the situation. I knew she wasn't attacking me so much as she was expressing her own feelings about a topic that was important to her. And even though I could rationalize that it was her interpretation of what I said and not the intent of my actual words, I still wasn't at peace. I decided to type an email in response, once again honoring her feelings so I could let go of mine. The moment I sent it off, I felt as though a load of bricks had been lifted from my chest. Once I pressed the send button, I let the issue fade from my thoughts.

Here's the lesson. We all mess up. The key is to address it as quickly as possible. Do everything in your power to make your peace. Do what you must so you can let it go. If you're not constantly releasing things that bring you tension or upset, you bottle them up, carry them around, and project them onto everyone else you come in contact with.

An employee of mine had been going through a tremendous amount of turmoil in his life. He had been dealing with a high-stress divorce and all of the change that comes with that transition. His "off" energy around the office was impacting several of his coworkers too. I had to confront the issue, no matter what it was, because his presence was having a negative impact on our workspace. I decided to call him and force the problem to the surface by telling him I wanted to play a game. His only responsibility was to be honest with his answers.

The first question I asked was "Where do you feel resistance in your life right now?"

"I don't know," he said. This is a typical answer from people who feel overwhelmed and are afraid to say what is on their mind.

"Listen, my friend. I know something is up because you're angry all the time. Anger is nothing more than a mask. Whatever you're re-

EXERCISE

Look at the seven most crucial areas of your life and make a list of any that are incomplete. See these incompletes as half circles just waiting to be closed.
They could include:

1. A call you've been avoiding.
2. A conversation you know you need to have.
3. Not expressing your feelings to someone who has upset you.
4. A project you've been wanting to do but haven't made time for.
5. Something you've always wanted to learn but never took the time to.
6. Someone you complain about all the time but never confront.
7. Health commitments you've made that you haven't honored.
8. The bill you're avoiding by not paying.
9. The savings account that is dwindling.
10. The contract that needs to be renegotiated.

These are just a few ideas to help you figure out the areas in your own life that need to be complete. With every one you complete, you close the circle and remove that piece of resistance from your life, thereby releasing yourself from the drama or upset that has been holding you back.

o o o o o o o

sisting is what's hiding behind your mask. So let's try to figure out why you're wearing that mask, okay?"

He agreed to continue, so I asked him about money, knowing that question usually elicits a response because most people worry about money.

"Oh, yeah, I definitely feel resistance with money," he said.

"Where else are you feeling it?"

"With my ex-wife." The gates were opening.

"And where else?" I kept probing, knowing there are always more areas to touch on.

"I feel it at work." Whoa. Remember, this was one of my employees, so I had to give him credit for honesty in that risky response.

"Is it with me?" I asked.

"Yes." I was stunned but relieved that he could get his feelings out in the open.

"Where is there resistance with us?" I sincerely had no idea what he would say.

There was a pause and then he said, "I love you and want to support our company, yet I realize you can only pay for a job and not the person doing the work. I spend all of my time with you visualizing, dreaming, and co-creating my future. I want to make millions of dollars a year, but my paycheck isn't in alignment with what I want."

When you find you're the person being confronted, the natural tendency is to fight or self-protect. Who was I, as the owner of the company, to stop anyone from achieving their greatness? Did I want him to leave the company? Of course not. But if you recall, I was in his shoes a few years earlier, so I understood exactly where he was coming from. If there had been room to grow within my organization, perhaps I could have offered him the chance to stay. Unfortunately, he was already at the top of his game and there was no more room to go. I was left with one answer to give him.

"Then you shouldn't be working for me anymore." My response

was quick but sincere. I wasn't firing him. I was setting him free from the resistance he'd been feeling and the animosity that was growing inside him every time he walked through our door.

"Let's figure out your strategy. Let me help you make a plan so you can achieve the goals you've set." We spent the next several minutes doing just that, talking about his future and what steps he needed to take to get there.

"I cannot believe I had been holding on to these feelings for the past several months. I didn't know how to say that you've led me down a path of 'extraordinary' and yet the work I do for you only pays 'ordinary.'"

Working for me was a boulder in his river. Once he removed it from the stream, everything began flowing as it should. A few months after leaving the company, he had a new job, met a fabulous woman, got married, and was living his dream.

If you don't deal with the issues that hold you back, they become like a pot of boiling water that eventually bubbles over. Once that happens, there's usually a giant mess to clean up, but then everything is better because nothing is still festering in the pot. You've got to release your negative emotions, remove the boulders that are impacting your life's flow. I call this getting back to neutral, the place I like to live where there is no stress and no worry.

I know that many of you have been extremely successful throughout your lives and are highly analytical and hard chargers. The focus of this book isn't about your career, though; it's about creating a balance in all the areas that make up the whole of your life.

The areas we will delve into together go beyond your outer shell. The explorations are designed to tap into your vulnerable side, a place that few people have the courage or ability to go on their own. I will push you to engage with your thoughts, your feelings, and ultimately the people around you. The questions you'll face throughout this book will most likely make you feel uncomfortable. If that happens, promise me you won't stop reading. I am not asking you to merely face your pain and self-imposed limitations. I want you to feel and be present with them so we can work on ways to ultimately let it all go.

> Pain is a sign that you're awake from your coma, so don't be freaked out by the feelings.

This chapter will help you explore your professional life, your lifestyle, and your health and vitality—the three main areas that make up your life. In addition, we will take a closer look at where resistance is showing up for you. As I mentioned in the Introduction, when I begin working with clients, phase one always starts with me asking questions about their lives so I can help them identify areas in which they've been living by default. Then we can start creating their By Design plan. Since you and I don't have the luxury of doing this in person, I have created my exclusive *Core Value Assessment* to help you gain insight and clarity about where default living is showing up for you.

EXERCISE

For the sake of the following exercise, I've purposely asked simple yes or no questions. These questions are designed to look for emotional triggers, so you can easily identify the areas in your life that need attention. Don't overthink or overanalyze your answers. Trust your gut and answer yes or no.

Professional

- Do you feel secure in your work?
- Does the economy worry you?
- Do you believe you are paid fairly for your work?
- Are you passionate about the work you do?
- Do you feel relevant to the needs of your marketplace?
- Are you current on technology?
- Are you clear on the value you bring to your organization and customers?
- Do you feel you are operating By Design in this area of your life?

Lifestyle

- Are you in a loving, passionate relationship?
- Do you have any unresolved issues with your parents?
- Do you have any unresolved issues with your siblings?
- Do you have any regrets about prior relationships?
- Are you satisfied with your outside interests from work?
- Do you give your children *real* quality time?
- Do you have an active social life?
- Are you having enough fun?
- Are you traveling as often as you would like?
- Are you grateful for where you live?
- Do you have powerful enriching feelings of faith?
- Do people seek you out to spend time with you?

- Do you feel you are operating By Design in this area of your life?

Health and Vitality

- Are you satisfied with your current level of energy?
- Are you satisfied with your physical appearance?
- Are you working every day to make your body the best it can be?
- Do you make excuses about your body?
- Do you play sports or participate in any athletic activities?
- Are you eating for energy, health, and vitality?
- Are drugs or alcohol impacting your work or personal life?
- Do you have high self-esteem?
- Are you moody or do you have mood swings?
- Are you happy?
- Do you suffer from anxiety, stress, or depression?
- Do you get tired early and often?
- Do you feel you are operating By Design in this area of your life?

STOP! How do you feel about each area we just questioned? What did you observe about your responses? If you were uncomfortable with your answers to these questions, you are not unlike most of my clients, successfully operating in some areas of your life but operating by default in others.

When I work one-on-one with a client, I look for any physical re-

> Now that you've read these questions, go back and write down your answers and how they make you feel. Is there someone in your life you should share your answers with? Are you up for more coaching?

actions they might have, such as a change in skin color, twitching, squirming, or any uneasiness; these are signs that we're on to something. If I am on the phone with someone, I might hear a long pause or several seconds of silence after I ask a question, which means he/she is being reflective or are inside his/her head, which is exactly where I want him/her to be. Did you find yourself going there when you considered the previous questions?

Anything that makes you feel uncomfortable needs to be addressed because it is where you're facing resistance—something incomplete. All change begins with discomfort. Awareness is the first step toward change. It's like being at an AA meeting where you stand up and say, "Hello, my name is Bob and I am an alcoholic." Saying "My name is Alice and I am incomplete with my relationship" is no different because it is an acknowledgment of how you feel. Those moments of uneasiness are when you are most likely to have your biggest breakthroughs.

A client named Jim was in a massive downward spiral in his business. When we first met, it took me a couple of coaching sessions before I got to the real reason he was so out of control. We spent most of our first session talking about why he thought he needed a coach, what brought him to my office, and where he wanted to go in the future. Our conversation was more on the surface and not as productive as I normally like to be during a first session. Either he didn't feel safe and secure, or I didn't create a strong enough connection or environment that would allow him to go to his deep, dark place.

The second time Jim came to see me, I was determined to get to the heart of his resistance. I wanted to know what he was afraid of. What was he hiding from his past that was keeping him stuck in this spiral? Whatever it was, I knew that the issue would need to be revealed before it ate away at his very being. I assured Jim that if we could figure out what that was, he would have a profound shift and an unimaginable life-altering experience.

"Are you up for that?" I asked. I know that a person has to *want* to go there, *want* to face those demons if we are going to slay them. Jim needed to be in the frame of mind to talk about the traumatic thing that happened or he would never trust me enough to reveal what he was hiding deep inside his soul.

"Tell me that dark secret, the thing that you've held back from everyone." I hoped Jim was ready. I told him to relax, close his eyes, and just speak from his heart.

"Tell me about a time in your early childhood when something happened. Something that really impacted your life." I had a hunch that whatever Jim needed to talk about happened when he was a young boy. Jim suddenly got choked up.

"Let it out, man. It's okay to cry." And he did for several minutes. When he finally caught a breath, I asked him to describe what he was seeing. "Don't just tell me about it. Describe it." The difference was that he would have to feel the emotion to describe the experience. That way, it wouldn't be just "words" he was speaking.

"I am in the living room of a house playing with my little brother. We had just opened up a large corrugated box. There was something in the box, but I can't remember what it was. I am holding the box upright so my little brother could climb on it. We were having fun, laughing, and just goofing around. And then, suddenly, he fell and hit his head. Everyone in the house came running into the room. The next thing I remember is an ambulance coming and one of the emergency techs telling my mother that my brother was dead. My mom looked at me and yelled, 'How could you have done this? How could you let your little brother die? You killed your brother.'"

I knew that Jim felt safe in my office telling me this story because he was no longer crying. He wasn't emotionalizing what he had just shared. I slowly brought Jim out of the relaxed, dreamlike state he'd been in so we could talk about that experience.

"My parents never forgave me, Tom. We were playing. He fell, cracked open his head, and died. It was an accident." Even though Jim called it an accident, he had spent the past thirty-seven years of his life convinced that in some way he had killed his brother. There was never a time when his mother or father told him it wasn't his fault. Their insistence that Jim killed their son was cemented so deeply in his consciousness that he believed it.

"How's your relationship with your mom today?" I was curious.

"We haven't spoken for twelve years." I wasn't surprised by his answer.

I spent the next twenty minutes talking to Jim about the impact this has had on every area of his life. We spoke about his relationship with his wife. I asked if she would say they have an extraordinary relationship.

"We're good, but I know I hold back from her, so we are not great." I assured Jim that I would probably be the same way if I grew up with that story imprinted in my brain. I asked Jim if he could step outside himself to look at the situation from a distance for a moment. I wanted him to remove himself from the story altogether.

"Would an innocent three-year-old boy playing with his one-year-old brother intentionally kill him?" I asked.

"Of course not." He was quick to respond. And yet Jim had lived his entire life believing that this was exactly what happened. I asked him several variations of that same question until he could sit in front of me and say, without any pause, that he did not kill his brother.

Breakthrough number one.

Before the end of the session, I asked Jim one last question. "How do you think your life would have been different if your brother was alive? What would your life look like today if he fell, your mom kissed the boo-boo on his forehead and put a Band-Aid on it, and then he went right back to playing?"

Jim had a blank look on his face for several minutes before answering. I am not sure he'd ever given that possible scenario any thought. "Wow, I don't think I'd have the edge that I have all the time. The constant guarded feeling I carry with me everywhere I go."

Breakthrough number two.

Jim had spent thirty-seven years carrying around the weight of his dead brother. His path in life wasn't to be a martyr. It was time to let go of his guilt and begin to live his life as it was meant to be.

For the first time since the accident, Jim was becoming free. He began to release all those years of guilt. We had a lot of unraveling and cleaning up to do to find the peace Jim needed and wanted, but that session was an excellent start.

When you look back at your own life, what old stories, true or false, have you reinforced and told yourself so many times that they have become your reality? Can you be present with one story right now? Maybe it's something that an adult said to you when you were a child, or something a peer once said to you. Perhaps your interpretation of something that happened became a story you kept close for years. How has that story affected the decisions you have made in your life? How has it impacted your relationships? And how can you release yourself from that pain so you can move on?

Once we addressed Jim's issue, we could do something about it. For him, this meant facing his mother after years of guilt and built-up anger for what happened. He told his mother how he felt and why he felt that way. He assured her that he was now old enough to understand that no parents would ever want to say something so hurtful to their own child, but in the heat of the moment, it is what he remembered her saying. His mother was dumbfounded because she didn't have the same recollection of that tragic day. She didn't recall saying any of those hurtful words to her son. That conversation set them both free.

Breakthrough number three.

Through that one coaching session, Jim was released from his past and was able to let go of a lot of the anger, resistance, and guilt that had been holding him back. Naturally, Jim's relationship with his wife and daughters grew stronger. He reconnected with his mom. His production at work increased. He began making more money, lost weight, got healthy, and, most important, was finally able to feel peace and joy. We dropped the pebble in the pond and watched the ripple effect it had on his life.

If you've ever planted a garden, you know that it starts out pure and beautiful. If you don't pay attention to the garden, though, it doesn't take long for unsightly weeds to block the growth of everything you spent so much time planting. The good news is that weeds can be pulled and your garden will once again flourish. The same is true for the pain and issues that create resistance in your life. They can be resolved with a little more knowledge and a new basis from which to make better decisions.

If you're feeling uncomfortable, we're on the right track!

EXERCISE

- What are some of your earliest childhood memories?
- What were your early experiences when it comes to re-lationships?
- Who were your most positive influences growing up? What made them so important to you?
- Who were your most negative influences growing up? How did they influence you?
- What are your earliest memories of money? How have they shaped your approach to finance?
- What are your earliest memories of your body, self-image, and health? How have they shaped the choices you now make when it comes to your current health choices?

Life By Design addresses areas you are living by default. Raise your hand and admit which areas you live by default and I will help you get it right. If you understand this concept, it's because you are willing to announce to the world that you have a problem and you're eager to do something about it. Most people can identify the effects of their issues, but I will lead you to the cause, the resistance, and the areas of default.

I love to break things down to get to the details and examine the minutiae. With that in mind, let's take an even closer look at your life with a virtual snapshot of what I call the "Core Seven." We live in a cause-and-effect world. What we give, we get, so when you look at these seven areas, try to be as honest as you can be with your assessment. Being anything else will keep you from moving forward. C'mon. This is just you and me here. No one else has to see your answers, so move forward with power, confidence, and vulnerability.

The first Core Value examines your level of satisfaction with your career. Perhaps you're considering making a change at work, have been thinking about going back to work, or have been recently laid off. What are your feelings about your career?

The second Core Value is about your intimate relationships. Are you satisfied with the way things are at home? Are you married but thinking about getting out of that relationship? Or are you single and wanting to be in a loving and committed partnership? Whatever your status, think about the impact it is having on all the other areas of your life.

Third up is finances, which is a monstrous category for most people, especially when money is tight. How much of an impact is financial stress having on your life, relationships, career, health, and others around you? Are you facing a crisis or ignoring it?

The fourth Core Value is about your physical health. Are you working out on a regular basis? Do you get at least thirty minutes of some type of exercise at least five days a week? Are you satisfied with your appearance, or do you dress to hide the excess weight you've been carrying around for far too long?

Fifth is spirituality. This category can mean different things to different people, so look at this as any belief you have in a higher being as well as the amount of time you spend meditating, reflecting, praying, and looking inward. It's about the quiet time you give your mind, freeing it from daily internal chatter and finding moments of real peace.

The sixth Core Value is called Contribution/Giving Back. For me, there are two kinds of people in the world: those who sit around and wait for something to be handed to them and those who go out and make a difference. These are the people who want to experience life

CORE VALUE ASSESSMENT

Using the following scale of 1 to 6, rate each of the Core Seven categories according to how you feel.

Career

1. Don't find any time for it
2. Depressed and feel I've hit rock bottom
3. Ready for a change
4. Creating a plan and starting to take action
5. I'm happy and improving
6. Extremely satisfied and open for more

Intimate Relationships

1. Don't find any time for it
2. Depressed and feel I've hit rock bottom
3. Ready for a change
4. Creating a plan and starting to take action
5. I'm happy and improving
6. Extremely satisfied and open for more

Finances

1. Don't find any time for it
2. Depressed and feel I've hit rock bottom
3. Ready for a change
4. Creating a plan and starting to take action
5. I'm happy and improving
6. Extremely satisfied and open for more

Physical Health

1. Don't find any time for it
2. Depressed and feel I've hit rock bottom
3. Ready for a change
4. Creating a plan and starting to take action
5. I'm happy and improving
6. Extremely satisfied and open for more

Spirituality

1. Don't find any time for it
2. Depressed and feel I've hit rock bottom
3. Ready for a change
4. Creating a plan and starting to take action
5. I'm happy and improving
6. Extremely satisfied and open for more

Contribution/Giving Back

1. Don't find any time for it
2. Depressed and feel I've hit rock bottom
3. Ready for a change
4. Creating a plan and starting to take action
5. I'm happy and improving
6. Extremely satisfied and open for more

Desire to Learn and Grow

1. Don't find any time for it
2. Depressed and feel I've hit rock bottom
3. Ready for a change
4. Creating a plan and starting to take action
5. I'm happy and improving
6. Extremely satisfied and open for more

and be in a continuous state of growth. The more you give, the more you're making a difference. This core value isn't necessarily about charity or financially giving back, although that would be a piece of this category. It could be about volunteering your time, mentoring a student, giving unconditional love, or simply doing small, everyday good deeds that can change the world around you.

The seventh Core Value is about continued education and your desire to learn and grow. How often do you read a book that impacts your daily routine? Are you keeping up with current events and attending seminars or workshops to enhance your performance at work, improve your relationships and your health, or become a better parent? How much time do you spend on your intellectual self?

Your answers to all of these questions will help you assess how you feel about the Core Seven areas of your life. This is critical to determining where we should focus your energies to move you from by default to By Design.

If your answers are primarily 1's and 2's, you are living by default. How does knowing this make you feel? Are you ready to change?

If your answers are primarily 3's and 4's, living By Design should come easily to you. You are in a good place to embrace change and improve the quality of your life from good to great.

If your answers are mostly 5's and 6's, you're already on your way to living By Design. But you're open for more, aren't you?

Congratulations! You've identified where in your life you're strong and the categories of your life where you experience resistance and struggle. Before we move on to the next chapter, I'd like you to write down next to each of the Core Seven why you answered the way you did. What are you present with by revealing your answers? If you're up for an immediate breakthrough, a huge aha, a barrier removed, or some resistance released, share your answers with someone you feel connected to.

Remember the exercise of completing all of your half circles (on page 43)? This is the perfect opportunity for you to become complete with some of those.

When you actually get down to doing the work in this chapter, I promise you will have tremendous breakthroughs that will start you on the right path to living By Design.

How are you feeling? Ready for more?

Turn the page.

FACE IT—YOU'RE ADDICTED!

Because the focus of this book is to quickly teach you the strategies to shift from living by default to By Design, the next step you'll need to take is facing your addictions. Before you raise your hand in total disagreement, let me explain what I mean. Everybody is addicted. Jack Canfield, coauthor of the successful *Chicken Soup for the Soul* series of books, has said that we are "a society of addicts." I completely agree.

Addiction is a state of psychological or physiological dependence on a habit-forming substance. It can also be considered anything in which you show a great interest and to which you devote a lot of time.

Okay, got it? Good, except, that's not what I'm talking about when I refer to addiction. I am not focused on drugs, alcohol, food, gambling, sex, or any other vice. To me, those are *symptoms* or *effects* brought on by four much larger *causes*.

If you're like me, you may know people who suffer from one of the addictions I mentioned above. As your coach, I want you to know *why* they do those things, *how* they got there, and some of the driving forces that brought those effects into play. I always want to go back to that specific day in their lives when they woke up and said, I'm going to take this, drink that, try this, smoke that, snort this, eat that, sleep with, et cetera.

I have a friend whose husband was involved in a terrible car accident that ended his career as a professional athlete. Depressed and unable to do what he loved most, he began drinking all the time until it was obvious to everyone around him that he'd become an alcoholic. His wife constantly made excuses for his behavior, saying he wasn't in control and had been stripped of his identity as a pro athlete the day he crashed his car. I tried to explain that her husband had choices about how he responded to the changes in his life. He chose to drink. He picked up the bottle all by himself and raised the glass to his mouth without anyone else's help. Still, she insisted it wasn't his fault, even going so far as enabling him to continue his drinking. That was at great cost because it caused the demise of his marriage, his relationship with his children, and any hope he had of salvaging something from his former career.

In this case, I can easily point to the day of her husband's accident as his life-altering event, the *cause* that brought on the *effect*, which was his drinking. But sometimes it's not that easy. In fact, most of the time it's pretty hard because breaking free from the addictions I refer to throughout this chapter requires a lot of soul-searching and honesty.

Most of us attach a lot of meaning to big moments in our life. These could include the death of a loved one, being fired, starting a new job, getting divorced, ending a relationship, beginning a relationship, having your first child, or having an unexpected pregnancy. The list is infinite and could include just about anything that happens along the course of life. Most of us create a "story" around a particular event and spin it over and over in our minds until it takes on a much greater meaning than the actual event itself.

For example, do you know someone who has been recently fired or whose job was eliminated because of corporate cutbacks? The moment they heard the words "You're fired," they likely began to fantasize about what that means. How will their spouse respond? How will they find another job? What if they can't find another job? How will they put food on the table, pay their bills, and meet other financial obligations? Our tendency is to spin those two words down a very negative path.

Most people naturally play out all of the worst-case scenarios in their heads. Those hallucinations are tied to something from their past that shaped and formed their response to what has just occurred. This stimulus response is tied to four primary addictions we all have and are the ones I refer to throughout this chapter.

Good or bad, experience shapes our values, which are our principles, our ethics, our moral code, and our standards. Our values create our habitual behavior, our routines, practices, and patterns. So here's what I want you to get: Who you are today is the sum of the experiences you've had, your beliefs about those experiences, and the stories you shared with yourself about those experiences, which in turn shaped your values and habits.

I'm asking you to consider the following:

If we are our habits, who created them?

If we are our values, who created those?

If we are the sum of our beliefs, *how can you change those to live the life you want?*

The four addictions I've listed destroy more dreams, more hopes, and more lives than alcohol, drugs, food, gambling, or sex combined. Living without joy and happiness is what forces us into that coma! These addictions are the *why* we will explore in this chapter.

1. *Addiction to opinions of others.* As a society, we're addicted to what others think about us and how others' views of the world affect us.

2. *Addiction to drama.* People are drawn to and consumed by any event or situation that occupies their thoughts and fills their mind with negativity, which often brings attention to them in unproductive ways.

3. *Addiction to the past.* People have an unhealthy attachment to events or situations that occurred in the past. They're stuck in how things used to be.

4. *Addiction to worry.* This addiction comprises all the negative and self-defeating thoughts that make us anxious, disturbed, upset, and stressed, that hold us back in life.

My goal is to help you identify the roles and impact of these four addictions in your life, and help you become more conscious of them—and know exactly what to do when they show up.

Although for some people addiction is a disease they're born with, a recent study showed that the propensity toward addiction is most likely formed from early childhood experiences. The study showed that events such as divorce, growing up in a single-parent home, lack of love and affection, or parents who suffered from addiction make a child more susceptible to becoming an addict.

I bumped into a good buddy while on vacation in Mexico. Although we weren't traveling together, our families hung out for most of the week we were there. Toward the end of the trip, I noticed that he hadn't had a single drink. I knew this guy had a passion for fine wine. We had talked many times about our favorite vintners. When I asked him why he wasn't drinking, he told me he'd given up all alcohol when his son was diagnosed with attention deficit hyperactivity disorder. He'd done some research and discovered that it was a natural progression for a child with this disorder to become an alcoholic. He and his wife decided that having liquor around the house would make it easier and more natural for their son to think it would be all right to have a couple of drinks, which could possibly lead him down a trail that his parents didn't want to be responsible for. To me, that's great parenting—and that's what it takes to break the cycle of addiction.

The same theory holds true for the four addictions from which we all suffer. It's all about cause and effect. My goal is to help you identify these four addictions in your life, become more conscious of them, and then create the change that will inevitably set you free.

Still not convinced of what I'm saying? Check out the following list. If any of the statements resonate with you, you're an addict.

ADDICTION

ADDICTION TO OPINIONS OF OTHERS

I became aware of addiction number one after a meeting with one of my most trusted and respected mentors, Bill Mitchell.

"If you were to die today," I said, "what's the most important lesson you'd want to pass on to your only granddaughter?"

He thought a moment before answering. I could see his eyes welling up as he pondered his response.

"Most people care way too much about what everybody else thinks. I have the most beautiful granddaughter, but whether *I* think she's beautiful, or somebody else *doesn't* think she's beautiful— neither of these things really matters. If she could understand that it doesn't matter what anybody else thinks about her, only what she thinks about *herself*, then I'd know in my heart that she'd be okay throughout her life. She will have the inner confidence to go out there in the world and do anything she wants."

Bill's inspiration made me consider other ways in which this phenomenon might manifest. I thought about fashion and why designer labels are so important to some people, and the importance of driving the right car or having the right address or title on your business card. It all boiled down to image and impressions.

Then I took my thoughts to the next level and began to wonder what stops an unhappy woman from leaving her husband or lover. To what extent is that decision inhibited by her worry about what other people might think or what the neighbors might say? Is she concerned about what her children or her parents will think? Ultimately, these questions come down to us looking for approval, and in some cases making sure we don't receive disapproval from others. The need for approval has been instilled in us from the day we were born. It is taught to us by our parents, grandparents, church, school, work, and most everyone we come into contact with on a daily basis. Society has put us into a place where approval from others is highly important. Approval from others gives us a sense of higher self-esteem. We're convinced that their recognition matters to our self-worth and how deeply we value ourselves. *We all want validation, but it is unhealthy if everything we do is strictly about getting it.*

There are two types of decision makers in the world. Internal decision makers self-analyze every step, every option, every possible outcome and never talk it through with others. They know what they know and don't need the opinion of others to validate their point. This doesn't mean they don't care about others' opinions. In fact, my experience is that it is quite the opposite. They've been burned so many times that their self-defense mechanism kicks in and they choose to make their decisions on their own as a way of avoiding rejection.

TOM FERRY'S THE SURE SIGNS OF FOUR ADDICTIONS

These are merely ideas to help you identify how each addiction could be showing up in your life. Do not reject the addiction if you don't relate to the six examples in each category. Think about situations in your life that might be more relevant to you.

Addiction to Opinions of Others

1. You are concerned about what others say or think about you.
2. You have good ideas and intentions but find yourself afraid to act on them.
3. You overleveraged yourself financially with cars, clothes, homes, jewelry, and more.
4. You are constantly seeking other people's approval or avoiding their disapproval.
5. You're afraid to speak in public.
6. You're afraid to speak your mind.

Addiction to Drama

1. You love to gossip.
2. You are always in the middle of a crisis.
3. You're glued to the news, magazines, and stories about others.
4. You tend to overreact rather than behave rationally.
5. You make things a bigger deal than they actually are.
6. You're a pot stirrer.

Addiction to the Past

1. You constantly talk about the past and the way things used to be.
2. You resist change.
3. You continually fail to plan for a better future.
4. You argue that things used to be better in the past.
5. You've allowed relationships to become stale, uninteresting, and without passion.
6. You behave as though you have physically and/or mentally peaked.

Addiction to Worry

1. You're depressed, concerned, and fearful about everything.
2. You spend time with other worriers.
3. You turn to TV and movies to escape the thoughts in your head.
4. You continually wake up at night from your mind chatter.
5. You think first of the worst-case scenario.
6. You use food, alcohol, or drugs to control your moods and feelings.

External decision makers constantly seek the opinions of others, asking for their approval in ways such as, "Do you like this idea?" and "Am I right?" "Does this dress look nice on me?" "Are we in the right place?" "Am I doing the right thing?" and "Are we okay?" They're thought of as team players because they want to get everyone involved in their process. They simply can't move forward without validation from others.

Consider this example. Have you ever come up with an idea that you thought was brilliant?

You said to yourself, "No one else has ever thought of this" and you're convinced you're going to make millions of dollars on it, right?

You tell your wife, best friend, boss, whoever is important to you, and they say, "That's a terrible idea! No one will ever buy that."

Wham! You've been stopped cold before you got your idea off the ground. What happened to the dream? It died on the table. There's no commitment, no follow-through, and no attempt to make it happen. You fall right back into your active coma and continue living a humdrum life. Someone else's opinion meant more to you than your dream. You placed a higher value on their opinion than on your brilliant idea. Imagine if the founders of Apple, Facebook, and Google gave up the first time someone told them "no" or said, "No one will ever spend that much time connecting with friends on a computer."

Several years ago, I ran a contest at one of my seminars offering one year of free coaching for the winner. Carol, a new realtor from San Diego, won the grand prize. From the moment we met, I knew she was destined to do something great.

Carol had just started selling real estate and wanted to improve her productivity. When we met, she had sold only three houses during the first seven months of the year, making barely enough money to support her family and cover her bills and obligations. She and I talked often even though she was working with another coach in my firm. It was important to me that she gain every possible edge during her year of free coaching. I made her success my personal goal.

Five months into Carol's coaching work, she asked me for personal advice. As I always do, I asked her to share her story with me. I wanted her to tell me about her parents, siblings, relationships, and children. She told me about her four kids, her unsupportive ex-husband and parents, and other personal struggles that she was facing. She wanted me to help her get on track while balancing her role as mother and coping with her unsupportive parents and the possibility of a new relationship, all while building her fledgling real estate career.

When I asked Carol, "Where do you feel the most resistance?" she immediately shared her parents' feelings about her decision to become a real estate agent. They told her it was irresponsible for her to leave a steady paycheck working as an accountant to get into the risky business of real estate. Even though she did it anyway, her parents continually reminded her of her mediocre success. Carol was clearly suffering from addiction number one. Like most children, even when they're in their forties, she was still seeking the approval of her parents. The conflict was that she recognized that her former job was a dead end. She had already taken it as far as she could go financially, and her desire to create a better life for her children was stronger than her anxiety about starting a new career.

Can you imagine being Carol—stuck between your vision and the desire to have approval from your parents? What would you have done? Add to this a declining real estate market, an uncertain income, constant struggles with her children, and trying to find a date too!

Carol struggled with her addiction to the opinions of others throughout the year we spent together. I had to slowly chip away at those layers, helping her to realize that her parents' intentions weren't bad; they were just trying to protect their daughter. They did the best they knew how, which was intended to be a continual expression of protection. Their vision was for her to play it safe. Unfortunately, it didn't match Carol's vision for herself. She needed to honor who her parents were but not take their words personally or let them hold her back. By the end of our year of coaching, Carol had learned to be aware of what her parents had to say and then file it in its proper place, giving their doubt no value and not letting it feed her insecurity.

Today, I am proud to say that Carol is still a client and doing well in real estate. She ran the San Diego marathon, dropped thirty-five pounds, and has done many things in her life to get closer to her overall vision of being an independent and successful provider for her family. And she has slowly let go of her addiction.

The addiction to the opinions of others affects areas of your life in ways you may not even be aware of. For example, your decision to live in a particular neighborhood, drive a certain car, send your kid to private school, wear only designer labels, take the "right" vacations, or join the "right" clubs are all tied to what someone else thinks. If you wear a Rolex watch or drive a Mercedes-Benz, is it because you love them or is it because you know that other people will see them as signs of success?

Ask yourself, "Have I overextended myself financially? Did I buy things I couldn't afford?" If the answer is yes, why did you make those choices? Chances are, it's because you've been playing a fierce game of keeping up with the Joneses—a sure sign you're addicted to the opinions of others.

I was introduced to John, a young entrepreneur, by a client of mine. The three of us met for lunch in Beverly Hills. John pulled up in an exotic sports car, flashed a diamond-encrusted gold Rolex, was dressed in the finest clothes, and was super bling. The three of us chatted to make our formal introductions before my client had to leave. Once we were free to speak openly, I asked John about his past and how he got to where he is today. He shared the all-too-common story of the kid from the other side of the tracks with divorced parents, always financially scraping by, dreaming that someday he could become a multimillionaire. As we talked about his business, his early success, and what became a rather excessive lifestyle, John told me that he never saw something he didn't want to buy. Whether it was the latest gadget, jewelry, clothes, or cars, he always had to have the newest and best of everything.

When I asked him "Why?" his response was simple.

"In my industry, people want to know that they're working with someone who is highly successful," he said with a cocky air of self-importance.

With his answer, I realized that John was suffering from a severe case of addiction to the opinions of other people. He had fallen into the worst trap. After hearing his story, I asked him why we were together and what he wanted to work on. He said his business had suffered considerable losses and his profits had become razor thin. I asked him what actions he had taken to improve sales or decrease his expenses and overhead, to which he said there wasn't much he could do because the majority of his clients weren't doing the volume of transactions they used to.

I asked, "What financial cuts have you made to accommodate your lack of income?"

His response was "I can't fire anyone because people will think my business is suffering."

"What about all of your expensive toys? Can you cut back or liquidate those?"

"I can't do that! If I did, people would know there's a problem!"

Can you see the trap that John was stuck in? His behavior was about impressing other people, which he believed fueled the perception of a successful business. John was being irresponsible by not cutting back on his personal expenses and business overhead. He was more concerned about his image than he was the welfare of his employees, his family, and ultimately his career.

I spent the rest of our lunch explaining that no one except you really cares about the stuff you have, the car you drive, the clothes you wear. I'm not saying that caring about those things is bad, but for some people it can be a turn off. I told John he needed to make tough decisions, and they had to be made at once. He would have to cut his overhead, which meant reducing salaries or terminating employees. He had to sell most of his "toys" so he could reallocate his assets to make it through tough times.

Up to that point, everything I said was basic common sense. The real coaching I gave John that day was that he wasn't the kid from the other side of the tracks anymore, nor was he all the excess he had accumulated. He was just like everyone else, doing the best he could to survive. If I could get him to see that what was holding him back was his attachment to what others thought, he would be able to more easily let go of his made-up identity and find his true self.

The addiction to what other people think has another significant impact; it represses us, which in turn keeps us in a sort of purgatory, afraid of the consequences of pursuing the life we really want. "If I do this, they will say _____." You won't be happy because you believe that people are judging you. It becomes easier to stay miserable so everyone else in the status quo will be fine. John was a perfect example of this kind of repression. So is the woman with the following story.

I have a client who was living in total denial about her sexuality. I kept telling her that her true potential was dependent on coming clean about being gay. Although a handful of close friends knew she was a lesbian, she still hadn't told her parents—something she had been avoiding for years. She worried that her folks wouldn't love her anymore if they found out. The truth was that her parents were well aware of her sexuality. She had had the same roommate for eight years. They surely noticed one king-size bed in the master bedroom and the small, never-used trundle bed in the guest room when they came to visit. And still my client insisted that her parents couldn't possibly know, and she felt it would kill them to find out she was gay.

I told her she had to address the elephant in the room. If she didn't have the courage to face the truth with her family, who was she as a person? I asked her if she was willing to wait for her parents to die before she could finally live her life free of this self-imposed shame and guilt. That question was the one that helped her see that she had to set herself free from all of those emotions.

She finally told her parents. Of course they knew, and told her, "We love you for who you are." Can you imagine the weight that was lifted from her shoulders and the stories that were released from her mind? She was free.

Because we are the stories we tell ourselves, they affect the way we behave. When we release ourselves from an old story, we let go of our self-imposed conversations and traps that keep us stuck. In the process, we become more sure of ourselves, doubt ourselves less, become more expressive, and are more likely to make decisions that move our life forward because we're no longer living from that story in our mind that has been holding us back. After my client came out to her parents, she no longer lived with her fear of being caught in a lie or living inauthentically, especially around the people who mattered most to her. When she wasn't being honest about her sexuality with her family, whether she was aware of it or not, she wasn't being honest in other areas of her life either. She certainly wasn't living By Design. And when you're living by default, you are worried about what other people think, living in constant drama and fear.

My client's ability to become complete in her life, not just with her parents but also with herself, allowed her to release from those areas that were holding her back. As a result, within a few months her production went up, her business was on its way to a new level, and her life blossomed. She realized that her relationship was no longer working, and subsequently fell in love with her soul mate. She has since found a balance and harmony in her life she never dreamed of achieving.

When I faced the difficult personal decision to leave my family business, I thought, If I leave, who will I be? A great deal of my adult self-image had been fostered and developed there. I worried what my wife would think if the money suddenly disappeared and I could no longer provide for our family in the same way. I worried what my friends would think if I had to sell our second home in the desert and they could no longer come for visits on weekends. Yet, with all of those questions, it wasn't until I asked one very important one that I realized what I needed to do: Why would I continue to stay in a situation that was making me increasingly miserable?

After many discussions with my wife and several mentors, I realized that the only solution was to do what was right for me, no matter the outcome. Of course, I also knew that I could not stay if I wanted to be happy. *When I was able to let go of caring about what other people thought and make my decisions free and clear of other people's opinions, I could easily make my decision and powerfully move forward on my own terms.*

I never feared public speaking, but I find it a common trait with many of my clients. When I ask them why they feel this way, most often it's because they worry about looking foolish in front of other people, especially their bosses or peers. Some also fear that their listeners will disapprove, criticize, or even walk out of the room when they are speaking. They get so nervous that they work themselves into a frenzy. Their palms get sweaty, their throat tightens up, their mouth gets dry, and they may even get light-headed just thinking about their presentation. Once they start talking, their voice trembles, their knees or legs shake, and they may stutter as they try to speak. This type of humiliation can destroy a person's ego and confidence. When I remind clients that the audience is generally on their side—after all, they're there to support and not destroy their vision—it takes away the power they've given to the people sitting in the room. This kind of fear is closely tied to an addiction to the opinions of others.

I recently saw an exceptional Nike ad showing clips of Lance Armstrong and other athletes during various phases of physical rehabilitation. The voice-over is of Armstrong repeating all the negative comments people made about him throughout his illness.

"They say I'm a doper."

"They said I would never get back on the bike."

The entire dialogue was negative and against this remarkable athlete until the last line, where he says, "I'm not back on the bike for them."

This commercial is a perfect example of having enough self-confidence to overcome the negativity of critics. Lance Armstrong is the epitome of someone who pursues his passion and doesn't give in to what anyone else thinks. His vision is making a contribution to this planet, to society, to his community, which makes him happy. He empowers countless others to follow in his footsteps, to believe in themselves, to never give up, and to live strong.

Still not convinced that you may suffer from this addiction? Try wearing a tutu to your office tomorrow or trading in your sports car for a bus pass. Stop going to the gym, getting Botox injections, coloring your hair, or getting manicures. Or imagine yourself doing something radical and potentially life altering, something you've been thinking about for years. Go home and tell your spouse you aren't happy and you feel that your relationship is in a coma. Walk into your boss's office and tell him/her you want more responsibility and more room for growth or you'll quit. And do it without worrying about the consequences.

The only way to have complete freedom from this addiction is to not care about the outcome. This is a lot easier said than done. It takes practice and courage to not place any level of importance on someone else's opinion. Remember, an opinion is not fact. It may not even be the truth. It is merely someone else's view about an issue that is based solely on personal judgment.

EXERCISE

How has addiction to the opinions of others shown up for you? What areas in your life are affected by what others think?

ADDICTION **#2**

ADDICTION TO DRAMA

The second addiction is an unhealthy attachment to drama, which is closely connected to addiction number three, addiction to the past. People love drama and often live for it. They can't wait to wade knee-deep in the excitement of conflict. Their entire identity is wrapped up in living in drama.

Do you know anyone like this?

Drama is created by your reaction to something in the past or present, or projected for the future. Here's a question for you: Now that you've experienced that moment, in the split second after it occurred, what did you make it mean?

I once heard the saying "Big stuff, you're born; big stuff, you die. Everything else is small stuff." Granted, the death of a loved one, divorce, being fired, and suffering financial setbacks are all big moments in life that can understandably cause you to feel upset. These traumatic experiences are all dependent on one thing: *the story we attach to them and the meaning and emotion we associate with the events.* I don't want to diminish their significance because they are very real. However, the common mistake people make when dealing with dramatic events is to allow themselves to get stuck in them. Most people feel victimized by these experiences and then use them as excuses to take time off, wallow in their misery, throw a pity party for their loss, or, worse, accept things as they are and continue to live by default.

Do you know someone who has suffered from one of these kinds of losses who never recovered?

Here's my stance. We're all the lead characters in the story of our lives. So, my question for you is, are you casting yourself as the victim or the victor? Victims give away their power, blame everyone else for their problems, and take no responsibility in their own lives. They don't see themselves as having any control over what's happening around them. Their perception is that there's nothing they can do. They call themselves "victims of circumstance."

When I think of someone who could have cast himself as a victim but chose to become a victor, I think of Captain Jerry Coffee, who lived in captivity for seven years during the Vietnam War in the infamous "Hanoi Hilton." He spent most of his time in solitary confinement, enduring unimaginable torture. Instead of breaking, Captain Coffee emerged with a strengthened faith in God, a love for his country and his fellow man, and a belief in working together for the common good. When I heard Captain Coffee speak several years ago, he described as "subtle" the differences between a survivor and one who just gives up. For Captain Coffee, it boiled down to knowing himself and understanding that he had the strength to endure his horrific circumstances and survive. His positive mind-set made him a victor in every sense of the word.

Another excellent example of victor versus victim is told in Dr. Viktor Frankl's book *Man's Search for Meaning,* which chronicles his experiences in a Nazi concentration camp and describes the reasons he continued living. Frankl was an Austrian neurologist and psychiatrist who had incredible insight and a fierce determination to survive while imprisoned. Even under atrocious circumstances—he was starved, kept in freezing conditions, endured brutal beatings, and lived with the presence and promise of death throughout the years he was imprisoned—Frankl found meaning in life and used it as a mechanism to survive.

Frankl recorded his findings and wrote about his observations after he was freed from the concentration camp. His theory was that finding something to live for gives us meaning in our lives. After spending years watching others give up, watching prisoners die every day, it got to the point where Frankl was able to determine who would make it and who would die among new groups of people who arrived at the camp. He could tell from their initial stimulus response to the Nazi camp leaders which prisoners had the mental strength and toughness, the reserve, belief, and faith that no matter what they had to do, they would survive.

Your life is your own story, so if you have the proper tools to handle adversity, you will have absolute control over how you respond.

"When we are no longer able to change a situation, we are challenged to change ourselves."

—Viktor Frankl

The responsibility falls on us to find meaning in our lives and make them worthwhile. Those who cannot find real meaning or purpose will chase gratification with desperate energy, as if they're trying to fill the emptiness inside their body, mind, and soul.

When people enduring hardship come to me, I try to get them out of their negative mind-set as quickly as possible by turning their thoughts toward creative, positive uses. When you feel good about things, you are free to create and express yourself. When you feel miserable, stuck in your addiction to drama, you're crippled with fear, panic, worry, and a sense of worthlessness. Think about it this way: When you are making lots of money, you feel as though you can catch a tiger by its tail, right? But what happens when you suddenly stop earning big bucks? If you're like most people, you stop feeling good, lose your creativity, and can barely get your head off the pillow in the morning. You may even be feeling this way right now.

The bottom line is this: How you feel determines your attitude. Your attitude then determines your actions, which ultimately determine the outcome. We don't act in our own best interests when we feel uncertain and insecure, when we feel that the world is ganging up on us. Are you one of these people? If so, consider, my friend, you're an addict.

When you live in drama, you're coming from a place where you have been living as a victim. There is nothing positive that comes out of that way of thinking. All you do is propagate negative energy into the universe. Keeping negative energy out there all the time, whether through dialogue, gossip, unnecessary conversations, self-talk, body language, attitude, or mind-set, is the epitome of living by default.

Why do so many people seem to feel comfortable in this place of conflict? There's a perceived benefit to being dramatic. We get attention. Our needs are being met because we are connecting with others. We get to be part of a clan because we can get everyone around us involved in our chaos. While all of this emotion is stirring, our need for interpersonal connection is being met by the person who calls to tell us some juicy gossip, by the person who brings up stories of the past, or by an email from a best friend who can't stop complaining about her abusive or empty relationship.

Perhaps you obsessively read tabloid magazines, feeding off every headline as if these celebrities are people you know. This too brings drama into your life. You are living off other people's drama and, worse than that, these are people you have never met!

I know a woman who had spent most of her life gossiping. I challenged her one day by asking, "Outside of your connections with friends, what benefit do you get from gossip? What benefit do you get from passing on negative information or bad news? I understand you feel connected to your friends, but is there another way you can achieve that same rapport?" She had never thought of her daily chats with girlfriends as damaging, but they were because they usually allowed the misery, misfortune, or negative circumstance from someone else's life to momentarily become a part of her own. She had become part of the problem by spreading the word.

Minidrama presents itself every day. It's unavoidable. I'm talking about getting stuck in traffic, a delayed flight, having a meeting canceled, or missing an important phone call. It comes when you're trying to get to your son's soccer game or get home on time for a wonderful meal your spouse worked on half the day for you. More modern-day drama might include impulsively sending an email you probably shouldn't have without first sleeping on it, or text-messaging, emailing, or befriending an ex on Facebook when it might upset your spouse if you're caught. All of these circumstances can create drama—if you let it. Your response to each of these scenarios will dictate the outcome.

A man walked up to me at a seminar and told me about a terrible car accident he was involved in four years ago. He stood before me crying that he hadn't been able to work or make any money since the accident because of his back pain.

As he spoke, I realized that:

He was at one of my seminars, so I knew he could leave the house.

He was walking, standing, and moving without any assistance.

He was telling me why he couldn't work.

I wanted to honor the fact that he had suffered a terrible injury, but I also wanted to grab him by the shoulders and scream in his face, "It happened four years ago! Get over it!" He was so stuck in the past and living in the drama of what happened that he couldn't get over it. He was obviously capable of finding work; he was *choosing* not to. He wakes up every morning talking about his hurt back and an accident that happened four years ago, which brings the drama from his past into the present and, unless he chooses to change, makes it his future. His alternative would be to wake up and say, "Four years ago I suffered a debilitating accident. Forget it. Today is a new day."

I have a dear friend who, after years of unsuccessfully trying, finally got pregnant. She was thrilled with her good news and had a relatively easy pregnancy. When the baby was born, she was told it was doubtful her child would ever walk. Although the diagnosis was grim, my friend never once asked, "Why me?" Instead, she said, "What can I do to make my daughter's life easier?" She took the birth of her daughter as a sign that she herself needed to slow down and just be present in her new baby's life. To me, that is the ultimate expression of being free from drama. My friend is an extraordinary mom who has spent countless hours doing physical therapy with her child, who, six years later, I am proud to say, can walk.

An unmet expectation also creates drama. You expected "A" but got "B." Your stimulus response is what creates the crisis. How you respond to the unexpected result will dictate the impact it has on your life. Here are a few examples of unmet expectations:

You're in line for a promotion and don't get it.

Your spouse planned a date night and the babysitter canceled.

You're leaving for vacation and your boss says the company needs you to stay.

You expected a bonus and got a fruit basket.

You can see where I am going here, right? When you have an intention and it doesn't work out, instead of sitting around, getting upset, or lashing out at someone or yourself, recognize that feeling bad about it won't change the outcome or solve the problem. So instead of getting caught up in the drama, create a new plan and get into action.

Have you ever noticed that when your spouse, co-worker, or best friend is in a bad mood, that can instantly change your mood? There are people who can change the entire temperature in a room simply by walking through the door. People with negative energy become what I've dubbed "energy-sucking vampires." You know who these people are. They walk into the room and the entire vibe changes. They kill all of the positive energy in their presence. When they leave, it's springtime again, right? What's worse is that they carry negative energy wherever they go. Everything about these people shouts "drama!"

Perhaps you've had long conversations with friends going through a traumatic time in their lives, where they pour their hearts out for hours until you're both so exhausted you can't take one more word of dialogue. They've sucked the energy right out of you, leaving nothing for anyone else, including yourself. These are energy-sucking vampires. These people require so much time and attention that they leave little room for anything else. Their lives are surrounded by drama all the time. They find that dwelling on hardship, problems, and the past is more interesting than being in the moment.

One of our jobs on this planet is to be a bucket filler for other people. We go around all day long, filling other people's buckets with compliments, support, guidance, and advice. It makes us givers of energy, hope, and optimism. When you fill someone else's bucket, you are encouraging them to be emotionally and mentally tough. Before you do that for anyone else, though, you've got to make sure your bucket is not empty, or you will be living totally by default. When your bucket is full, there's no room for anyone else's negativity to sneak in.

I declared a long time ago that I am a drama-free zone. Don't get me wrong, I still argue and disagree with people, but I don't let these moments blow up into something bigger than they are. I talk it out and put it to rest. Done. I help people try to move through their own drama, but I am extremely aware of not letting their negativity into my life. Do I sometimes have to absorb their energy? Yes, but I keep my bucket full enough that their negativity flows right out. There's no room for their darkness to seep into my world.

Over the years, I've slowly disassociated from people who brought constant drama into my life. Why? Because I want to surround myself with people who understand that living in drama impacts all areas of our lives. These are the "half fullers" of the world. They are not controlled by circumstance but recognize they can control how they respond.

These days, I am so By Design in my relationships and whom I choose to spend my time with that there are no energy-sucking vampires in my life. This is true for the people with whom I work, live, play golf, travel, socialize, and coach. If someone brings unexpected drama into the fold, I call them out and give them a set time to deal with it, or they can't play in my sandbox anymore.

Everyone has positive and negative habits. Habits are learned, which means they can be unlearned. Yet they are powerful and are reinforced by the people we surround ourselves with. Think about this: Some people find that having a workout buddy makes it easier and more motivating to go to the gym every day. It's much easier to stay out of drama when you surround yourself with people who don't live

in drama. They don't gossip, aren't always in the middle of a challenge or a crisis, aren't glued to the evening news, find no significance in other people's upsets, and don't blow everything out of
proportion. They recognize life's bumps as just that—momentary
hiccups.

EXERCISE

List all the people in your life who are energy-sucking
vampires.
Here's something to think about: Would you be on someone's vampire list?

The hardest part of letting go and releasing from an addiction to
drama is that, as with any addiction, most people get some form of
pleasure from the very things that are not good for them. The reality
is that, in life, drama will always be around. You can't escape it. But
you can choose to not let it consume you, and you can control the
meaning you give it. That's when drama can actually become powerful and productive because sometimes an unmet expectation is exactly what you need to change your course for the better.

My wife and I took our sons on a trip to Hawaii when they were
babies. We flew six and a half hours across the Pacific, and landed on
Maui. I had spent weeks planning the trip to make sure every detail
was taken care of so we could enjoy our seven-day family vacation.
We chose to go during one of the busiest weeks of travel to the is-
lands, so snagging reservations for our flights and hotel was nothing
short of miraculous.

When we got to the hotel, we were met by the staff with leis and the warm aloha spirit of Hawaii. I approached the front desk to check in, already sinking into my much needed vacation.

"Hi, Tom Ferry checking in," I said.

The clerk behind the desk tapped away on her keyboard, looking for our reservation. She kept tapping, and tapping, and tapping until she looked up and said, "Mr. Perry?"

"No. Mr. Ferry."

"Oh." She responded in a way that made me nervous.

My one-year-old son was now crying because he needed a diaper change, and my three-year-old was practically laid out on the lobby floor, desperate for a nap.

"When did you make your reservation, sir?"

My blood pressure was quickly rising because I suspected that what was coming next wouldn't make me happy. "I made the reservation weeks ago," I said, gritting my teeth.

"I'm sorry, sir. I have no record of your reservation."

Now, I could have gone ballistic and begun to yell and scream at the woman behind the counter, but what good has that ever done? I stopped, took a deep breath, and realized, What's the worst-case scenario here? I'm in Hawaii with my family. There's got to be a room somewhere on the island.

I put a tiny smile on my face and asked the woman if there was anything else available or if she could recommend another hotel.

She told me to hang on for a minute while she checked on options. She returned five minutes later and said, "Mr. Ferry, I have good news. The general manager would like to upgrade you to the presidential suite for the same price you were paying for the other room, and tonight's dinner is on us for the inconvenience."

Because I didn't overreact but remained calm and understanding and open to what was next, the woman behind the desk was more inclined to do something nice to help us out. She could have come back to say there was nothing available. Instead, she offered up the most expensive room in the hotel to rectify a situation that otherwise could have been disastrous.

So what's the lesson here? How we choose to respond to the unmet expectations and drama that are everywhere will dictate responses and outcomes. So the next time you are met with an unexpected situation, stop, take a breath, and remind yourself that everything has a way of working out.

A good friend named Claude is one of the happiest people I have ever met. He lives totally drama free because he chooses to live By Design. When I asked him how he stays out of the drama, he explained that he sees life as a movie. If we can see each moment as nothing more than a scene, before you know it, the next scene will be up on the screen and the previous moment of drama will be in the past. This analogy is a simple way to see every moment, good or bad, for what it is: a moment in time that will soon pass.

So, here's your assignment. Give up drama for the next thirty days. Stop making everything mean more than it is. See things as they really are. Try to create a better story around the events that happened in your life. Once free of the addiction of drama, you come from a place of peace. You will be able to recognize that *you* create your own certainty. There's an enormous amount of joy and happiness when you live in peace. When you let go of allowing your circumstances to dictate your outcome, you will be in control of your destiny.

Speak more life into your vision and the visions of others rather than focusing on your mistakes or drama from the past or present.

ADDICTION #3

ADDICTION TO THE PAST

Understanding—and letting go of—your past is the key to unlocking your future and your greatest potential. I know you've heard this before, and yet—perhaps reading this book now—you can recognize that this attachment to the past is an addiction. Many people suffer from it. Many of us live our lives stuck somewhere "back when," fixated on days—or people or circumstances—gone by. For some it's a love lost, a regrettable choice made; for others, perhaps it's being unable to shake free from a sense of obligation to parents or friends who are holding them back; or the lingering shame or guilt of something that happened in the past. Whatever it is, an addiction to the past is holding you back from living your best life.

When it comes to the past, we all have emotional balloons inside us that we need to let the air out of. We are habitual beings, so most people live their lives in the past because it has become a conditioned routine. Early in my professional career, I suffered from addiction to the past because I was stuck in a conversation with myself about barely finishing high school and not attending college. There used to be a constant dialogue going on in my head about whether I was smart enough to be teaching, educating, reprogramming, and helping others with their lives. Of course, I know that intelligence isn't about how many diplomas you have on your wall or how many letters follow your last name. I used to think that people would see my lack of degrees as a lack of qualifications to do my job. Of course, today, if I find myself momentarily worrying that Ivy League graduates might attend one of my seminars, men and women who may be smarter than I am, I now know that the main difference is that they got a shot at achieving success faster than I did. If I could make a success out of my life, I figure most anyone can make a success of theirs.

It has taken me twenty years to get here, but when I realized that the past is nothing more than a story we tell ourselves, it helped me understand that continuing to tell that story, verbally or nonverbally, eventually turns it into a reality. What you speak, you breathe life into, which cements those thoughts into your emotions. If something from my past presents itself, I choose not to talk about it. I don't fantasize about it and let it fester as a thought in my head. I remind myself that it is only a story, and I don't allow it to impact the moment. I'm an extremely mentally tough guy, but I didn't get there overnight. Getting there takes time, practice, a willingness to be strong, a vision for where you want your life to be, and then doing whatever it takes to get there, which I discuss at length in Chapter 7.

A client of mine is a twenty-three–year veteran in sales, a peak performer in her industry. She is extremely well respected and a nice person too. She's been selling for her company so long that she has become satisfied with her annual production, which hasn't changed much over the years.

By most people's standards, she's extraordinary. Of course, when you work with me, I expect more. What was stopping her from improving her results was her twenty-three years of experience. Okay. Let me say that again. Her past experience was actually holding her back from increasing her sales. Why? She knew how hard she'd have to work to up her numbers. She recognized the several more hours a week and all of the sacrifices it would take to kick things up a notch. She worried that she was too old and wasn't a good enough manager to lead her team to the next level. Why did she think this? She had so many stories built up in her head about her past that she believed she was at her maximum output and would be better off keeping things as they were. If she wanted to increase her productivity, the only way she knew how to do it was how she had done it in the past. She knew she'd have to spend more time at the office than she already did, keeping her away from her family and friends even more hours. She'd have to become more ruthless than she already was. And the amount of work required to rebuild herself, her skills, and her business systems was overwhelming since she had already been at the top of her game for so many years. She resisted anything that would require change or disrupt the way she had always done things, which kept her exactly where she had spent the past two decades. Comfortable, but stuck.

To some degree, we all suffer from addiction to the past. If you've been to a high school reunion, you recognized it there, right? You saw the star of your football team, the cool guy everyone wanted to be like, who clearly peaked in high school. Ten, twenty, or more years later, he's still walking around like the big man on campus.

Or how about the guy who never made much of himself in high school who now has kids of that age whom he vicariously lives through by pushing them to succeed at levels he never did.

I worked with a man who was unable to make the basketball team when he was a kid who now pushes his son to excel in the sport. Because he was living through his child—attending basketball camps, going to other team practices to see what they were up to, spending hours each night on the Internet to review what was happening in the sport—he disconnected from his wife. Obsessed with getting his son to play the game at a level he was never able to, he no longer had the time or desire to give his wife love, attention, affection, or anything else that makes for a quality relationship. As they disconnected, he turned to the Internet to look up old girlfriends and high school buddies, trying to reconnect and share his son's success as if it were his own. Everything he did was rooted in his past need to be accepted. Eventually, feeling abandoned, his wife had an affair and divorced him. He quickly remarried and repeated the same mistakes because he couldn't let go of his notion that his life used to be so much better back when, which of course, wasn't true.

What do these two stories have in common? Both people were resistant to change. They were so mired in who they used to be that they never evolved into something more. They're stuck in the past, so they can't become present in the here and now, let alone think about creating an exciting future.

Do you know someone who is stuck in the past? Is there an area of your life where you suffer from this addiction?

There's a line in *Fiddler on the Roof* where someone asks, "Why do we play the violin on the roof?" The answer was one word, "Tradition!" Great theory, but not all traditions are good. You can tell your children not to drink alcohol, but if they grow up watching their mom and dad throw back a few beers or glasses of wine every night, that is what they see and experience and are programmed to believe is the way things should be. If you grew up in a family where loud arguing and physical or mental abuse were everyday occurrences, chances are your home today is similar to the one you grew up in. We are all products of our past and present environment; however, it is our past experiences that shape our core values and ultimately who we become.

When *you* think about *your* past, where is there resistance? Are you happy with how you're operating, viewing everything from the past versus from a clean slate, looking forward?

When you look back on your life, what events do you recall having a tremendous impact on how your future was shaped?

Where in your life do you still feel a negative emotional tug? Perhaps you long for an ex-lover, have unresolved issues with your family, or live with regret for past actions. Whatever it is, my advice is to get it cleaned up.

Cleaning up the past is the simple act of facing it. You've got to fully recognize that if you stay on this path, you will likely continue to go through life miserable. This is the course you're on if you remain addicted to the past. You cannot find joy. You won't find peace and happiness if you are firmly planted in old resentments, old boulders, old challenges, old stories about your health, your vitality, your income, and past relationships that have gone awry. If you keep telling yourself these same old stories, all you will have is conflict.

If you are still holding on to the day you were fired, were rejected by a lover, did something wrong, had something wrong done to you, were hurt by someone, or made a terrible mistake, you're haunted by those memories and are addicted to the past. If you think you're unhappy now, think about your life ten years from now if you choose to do nothing and remain the same. Now amplify those feelings times twenty years. Knowing what you know about your past, are you willing to let it go and work toward planning a better future?

Star athletes are trained to let go of a loss the second a game is over so they can move forward and into their next game, match, tournament, or competition without bringing their mistakes with them. Imagine the discipline it takes to let go of those errors and not carry them forward. Granted, the athletes can go back and review the errors they made, but they cannot hold on to the emotion of the loss or they will lose their competitive edge. The past is behind them. All they can do is look forward to doing better in the future.

Addiction to the past most often shows up in how it negatively impacts people's relationships. Someone who suffers from this addiction will carry forward every fight, every mistake, every hurt feeling, and all of the other negative stuff that happens in relationships.

I know a woman who spent most of her married life with a man who avoided coming home at night and spent most of his time drinking with his friends. One day she woke up and decided she no longer wanted to live that way. She told her husband, "I've been with you for more than a decade. We can either make it great from here on out or we can go our separate ways."

I found her courage powerful and inspiring because she was willing to let go of all her anger and resentment from the past for a chance at a wonderful future with the man she had fallen in love with. The alternative would have been to suffer through the rest of her life living exactly the way she'd been—miserable and alone.

If your happiness isn't a good enough reason to let go of your past, think about your family, your spouse, partner, boyfriend, girlfriend, children, and friends. How have the events from your past impacted them? How you behave and act is what your kids will grow up emulating. By continuing to hold on to the past, not only are you destroying your own life, you are crushing the lives of all those around you. Whether you are the leader of your family as a husband or wife, or as a twenty-five-year-old single guy or girl hanging out with your friends, every one of us has our own moments of leadership. If you choose to go down a path being stuck in how your life used to be, the people around you will go down that path too. You'll be leading them to the deck of the Titanic if you choose to live in the past. You can choose to go down with the ship, or you can grab a lifeboat, load it up with your loved ones, and say, "Let's go create something new," and get over it together.

Getting over it isn't about forgetting. It is about accepting things for what they are. It's about coming to an understanding that what already happened doesn't need to be part of your present or future. The only way I know to reconcile the past is to confront all your areas of resistance. With loved ones addicted to the past, have conversations that start with you saying, "You need to resolve something," and then have the courage to honestly speak what's on your mind.

You can write a letter or an email to that person. Some people choose to actually send their letters, while others write them just to express their feelings and get their emotions off their chests. If you don't want to send the letter, burn it. Light it on fire and let your negative attachment to the past turn to ash with the paper.

When I asked my client Jim to face his mother about his little brother's death, it was about helping Jim come to terms with what happened so he could let it go and move on. I had him visit his brother's grave site, where he could let out all of his bottled-up emotion. I wanted him to say his peace to his brother, acknowledging out loud what really happened, how much he loved him and wished they were together today. These two actions were a huge breakthrough for Jim because he had shut his parents out at such a young age and now, because of that, he struggled with connecting with his own children on the deepest level. Once he cleaned up the past with his mother and the death of his brother, he could resolve the issues he faced at home with his own family.

If you want to be free from your past, let all of the people you name in the exercise below know how you feel. More times than not, you may be surprised that they have no idea what you're talking about. What made an indelible impression on you turned out to be meaningless or of little concern to other people. They simply had no clue you'd been holding on to all of that negative emotion, which ultimately weighed you down with self-created images of something that may or may not have happened.

EXERCISE

Write down a list of every person you feel you've wronged.
Write down a list of every person you owe an apology to.
Make a list of everyone you feel has wronged you.
Write down a list of every person you feel you deserve an apology from.

I have a client named Lana whose business had hit a plateau. No matter what she did to improve her performance, she couldn't get her earnings to a new threshold. As we worked together, I asked her to talk about events from her past that were related to her outlook toward money. It didn't take long before she revealed this telling detail. When she was a little girl, her parents had made an enormous amount of money, and then unexpectedly lost it—not once but twice. These losses were traumatic in ways she wasn't aware of until, after two painfully hard and emotional coaching sessions, we discovered that her fear of becoming too successful and then losing it all, just as her parents had done, was inhibiting her. Subconsciously she had convinced herself she was better off just getting by than she would be if she grew her business to its potential.

Lana's situation is something many people struggle with: As long as we place a negative label or story around success, it will always elude us.

Lana and I worked together to create a new association around the meaning of success. More important, I helped Lana accept that what happened to her parents was just that—something that happened to her *parents*. Their circumstance did not need to dictate her own. And the happy ending to this story? After exploring and letting go of her associations from the past, Lana more than doubled her income over the next twelve months.

The people who are really suffering and held up by their addiction to the past are those who cannot or choose not to see things for what they are. They see only their breakdowns, mediocrity, and failures and relate them to those in the past. Sometimes they get so caught up in prior choices that they risk everything to try to change the outcome.

A client came to me with a business idea that I believed would not work. It wasn't that he couldn't make the business a success; there were just too many conditions in the market that could cause failure.

The risks simply weren't worth taking. Despite my advice, he was sure he could create a successful company, make it profitable over the course of three years, and then sell it, move on, and create something new. It wasn't that I didn't believe in his vision. I couldn't support his vision because of what I knew about the market. As his business coach, I told him I thought he was setting himself up for disaster. He fired me on the spot.

A year or so later, he came back to me asking for help with his business because it turned out that I had been right. I didn't like being right, but I'd had the clarity and ability to see things as they were from the start. When he came back to see me, he wanted me to either help him take the company to the next level so he could build it up, or just make it saleable so he wouldn't lose the money he had in it. I agreed to take him back as a client because I've always admired him.

Our first order of business was to create a new vision for what he wanted to achieve. We spent the next eighteen months trying to bring that vision to life, but it didn't work. The market was tumbling, his profitability and margins were shrinking, and he was battling his addiction to the past—the fact that everyone told him that his company could not work. He was holding on to all the conversations he had when he first started his company, and that doubt was holding him back. He wasn't seeing things as they were because he was on a sinking ship while focused on a vision he created three years earlier to build something saleable in a marketplace that was now virtually nonexistent.

I told him it was time to begin transitioning to his old career, which was sales, because that was where he knew how to make money. As hard as it was, he reluctantly relinquished his role as CEO of the company, agreed to hand over control to his two other partners, and got back into the sales field. This was the only viable way I could imagine he could make the company valuable enough to sell for what he had in it. At best, I believed he'd get out without it costing him anything more than he'd already invested.

A few months later, his partners offered to buy him out. His asking price was the $600,000 investment he had in the company. When he called to ask my opinion, I told him he'd be lucky to get out without any further obligations. I didn't think the company was worth the money he was asking, and I was certain his partners knew it too. He could walk away free and clear and move on. That was my advice.

He was extremely resistant to what I had to say. Despite the failure of the company, he was still caught up in his original vision that he had to turn a profit and make the business a success. Now, I was suggesting he walk away from that vision and leave $600,000 on the table. Forty-five days and seven coaching calls later, he *still* didn't see things as they were. I had grown frustrated with him, which is never a good sign for a coach. As a last-ditch effort to bring him around, I related a scenario I came up with that I thought would help him see the light.

"The FBI and the IRS walk into your office tomorrow and they handcuff you. They've got your wife and children in front of you. They turn to your wife and say, 'We've caught him embezzling, committing fraud, and cooking his books. We're going to lock him up and throw away the key.' You're done, my friend. Now, can you imagine this happening?" I asked.

My client looked confused and said, "Do I have to?"

"Yes! Imagine how you would feel in that moment if you knew your entire life was being taken away. Whether you did those things or not doesn't matter. You're watching your children and your wife walk out the door as you're being led away in handcuffs. How would you feel in that moment?"

"Stop. I don't like it. I don't ever want to feel that way."

"How much money would you spend in that moment for your freedom?"

The answer was obvious. "Six hundred grand," he said sheepishly.

"You got it! You have been fighting with your partners to pay you six hundred thousand dollars they don't have for a company that isn't worth it. You're trying to help them get lines of credit they'll never be approved for. You're the most stuck person I coach. Your resistance is blocking your ability to see things clearly. The moment this thing is behind you, you'll be free to get back out there and do what you love most and make the money you deserve. And when you get that boulder out of your river, my friend, you'll thrive. You'll be back to making a couple of million dollars a year. This will be a blip on the screen. But until you let go of the past, you will live there. So, what's it going to be?"

My client got it right away. He realized he'd been living in a self-imposed prison, under lock and key, as if he'd been under house arrest. He wasn't able to live up to his vision because he was trying to recoup a bad investment and hold on to a vision that hadn't worked from the start. He called his partners and said, "You can have it all. I will give you everything." The second he did that, the 600,000-pound gorilla released him.

A few weeks later, he called to tell me that our coaching session paid for all thirteen years of our coach-client relationship. His big breakthrough hadn't been letting go of the money. He realized he hadn't been present to *anything* in his life while that situation was stirring. He hadn't connected with his wife in months, hadn't spent any quality time with his children, and realized he'd been so stuck in the past that there was no way to be in the moment. "I would spend every dollar I have to be free with my wife and children," he said, right before telling me he was taking the next three months off to reconnect with his family.

The benefit of freeing yourself from the past is that you can finally see things as they really are and not how you thought they were. Reality is reality. If a tree falls in the forest, believe me, there is noise.

Your interpretation of a story and the constant retelling of it set the tone for how that story will live in your life.

Letting go of your past empowers you to make new and better decisions for your future. There's a great advantage in knowing that.

So, what old stories are you holding on to that are stopping you from living your best life, By Design? How are these stories impacting your life? In what ways are they holding you back? And now that you are aware of them, what will you do to let go of them so that you can free yourself of self-imposed traps?

ADDICTION  #4

ADDICTION TO WORRY

The fourth addiction is addiction to worry, or what I refer to as "living with the drunk monkey." I first heard this description on an audio program by famed parapsychologist Dr. José Silva. During his talk, Dr. Silva said, "Negative self-talk is the equivalent of letting a drunk monkey loose in your kitchen. In the end, all you're left with is one big mess." That perfectly describes the power of negative self-talk, which is what fuels all worry.

The human mind has tens of thousands of thoughts a day. Experts estimate that the range is somewhere between 50,000 to 70,000! And guess what? Most of them are negative. We battle thoughts of doubt, lack, limitation, worry, fear, and death, to name a few. And we continue these same thoughts over and over like a continuous loop in our minds, which appear to be naturally wired to go to bad places. We've been conditioned to survive by fear, worry, cynicism, and skepticism. What is the value in that kind of thinking? What do we gain, if anything?

From the earliest age we're told, "Don't talk to strangers," "Look both ways before you cross the street," "Be afraid of barking dogs," "You'll get hurt," and "Don't go into the park at night." We interpret things based on our experiences, values, and habits. We've been conditioned to believe that most things in life are a little scary. Our reaction is habitual, and we are unaware of it until it's too late. We have a tendency to go back to our mental filing cabinet, our old experiences, and, like it or not, rehash the past. This response shapes our emotions and thoughts in any particular moment. During my live seminars, I ask participants to look at the person to their right and say, "Your head is a scary place to be." Everyone always laughs, but that statement is so true.

Have you ever wondered what your life would be like without worry?

How much bigger would your life and experiences be if you weren't worried about failure?

How would you respond to things if you couldn't worry about the outcome?

Imagine walking down a dark alley with zero fear, or meeting the person of your dreams and having no hesitation or apprehension of being rejected or hurt. That's a powerful possibility, isn't it?

My wife and I took a trip to New York City several years ago. She grew up in Southern California, so her only image of Central Park was what she had heard on the news—not even recent news, but the old stories to stay out of the park at night, that it's a dangerous place where people get raped, mugged, and murdered. My goal on that trip was to get Kathy over her fear of Central Park. One night after dinner, I suggested we walk back to our hotel by cutting across the park. She reluctantly agreed. As we strolled, I explained to her that if she fed her fear, she would never be able to enjoy the beautiful setting. Suddenly, I could feel Kathy's body tense up as her hand tightly clenched mine. She noticed a large man quickly walking right toward us wearing an overcoat and a baseball hat pulled down over his eyes and face. I could feel her trepidation as he approached. As he got closer, I suddenly realized it was the actor Andy Garcia. My wife was freaking out thinking he was a mugger, when it turned out to be someone whose work we both admire. Imagine the difference in her experience that night if she had been free from her preconditioned worry and assumption of a worst-case scenario.

I read a story about Ted Turner in his book *Citizen Turner* that I've never forgotten. The book tells the story of Ted's family. One morning, Ted's father kissed his wife on the forehead, turned to Ted, gave him a kiss too, and told them both to have a nice day. Before he left the house that morning, he said he forgot something upstairs. He disappeared up the steps in their family home, took out a gun, and killed himself. The story goes on about how he had been unable to handle the emotional stress of the many mistakes he had made in the family business. Although Ted was a young man, this is when he began to handle the family business so his mother didn't lose everything. He was dealing with the banks and other business interests to turn around the family fortune. He developed a survival strategy in life, which was basically to go for everything you want. There was no room for worry because the worst-case scenario was that he could always kill himself. He told bankers they could give him the necessary loans or he would just kill himself and they'd be left with a bunch of bad debts. Although his approach was extreme, it helped Ted build his empire from the ground up. Ted Turner was willing to accept the worst-case scenario, which not only kept him alive but helped him thrive.

I often talk to my clients about worst-case scenarios to help them understand that every challenge we go through in life is temporary. Circumstances do not define us. How we handle them does.

A client of mine was on the verge of losing his job. He was panicked at the thought of being unemployed. I took him through a series of questions so he could play out all of his worst-case scenarios prior to anything actually happening. When I asked why he was so upset about being fired, his first response was that he would lose his house. He was already on the brink of financial disaster and was a banana peel slip away from bankruptcy. If he lost his job, he'd never be able to make his mortgage payments.

"And if that happens, what else will happen?" I asked.

"The house will go into foreclosure. The bank will come and take everything."

"And if that happens?" I asked.

"I'll lose my wife. She'll divorce me and take what little I have left in this world."

I kept going because I didn't think we'd hit the worst case yet. "What would happen if your wife divorced you?"

"I'd lose my kids too."

"And if that happened?"

"I would die. I wouldn't want to live."

I looked at my client with a straight face and said, "So, let me get this right. If you lose your job, you will die? Like six feet under, die?"

My abrupt approach startled him at first. But then he realized how absurd he sounded. He wouldn't kill himself over losing his job. I explained to him that his worry had blown his possible job loss way out of proportion. Unfortunately, my client did end up losing his job, but only a couple of weeks later he was offered an even better job for significantly more money. In the end, his worry had been for naught.

People get overwhelmed because they cannot control their thoughts. I tell my clients that when this happens, they are actually underplanned—they haven't taken the time to get all the thoughts

EXERCISE

Write out a list of everything that worries you. Write down every negative thought in your head that makes you feel emotional and afraid. Take your list to a close friend, loved one, or someone you respect and tell them you'd like to read them the list of things you worry about. See how they respond. Do they think your fears are valid, or do they say you have nothing to worry about? Let them be your voice of reason.

Second, read each item on your list and ask yourself, using a scale of 1 to 10, "What is the likelihood of this ever happening?"

out of their head and onto a piece of paper. Once they can visually see what they're up against, they plan appropriately.

A client named Carol called me from her car, frantic and panicked. I could hear her whizzing down the highway in her convertible.

"I just can't take it anymore!" she screamed into the phone.

When I asked her what was going on, she rattled off one thing after another.

"My business is going full-tilt boogie. My daughter is about to get married, and I'm in the middle of a divorce. I need to stay engaged in my business, I'm dating a wonderful guy, and I'm thinking of moving. But before any of that, I need a vacation!" It was clear that the wedding and divorce were overwhelming her. She began to cry as she wondered how she would be able to walk her daughter down the aisle without her husband. I let her cry it out until it was time to step in.

"Are you ready to hear what I have to say, Carol?" I didn't wait for her to answer. I kept talking, hoping she would hear me.

"There is no more worry. You're overwhelmed, which means you're underplanned. So, let's get back to your list and create a strategy to get you through each layer of stress." I took all of the worry and drama and put it into a plan for action to make the weeks ahead less daunting. I told her that simply acknowledging the stress and overwhelming worries puts the brakes on them. But talking about it isn't enough. Making decisions about what is real and what needs your time and attention is key to removing a worry from your life.

A big part of my job as a coach is bringing each client's vision to life by talking about it as if it has already happened. I believe in their possibilities. I set high expectations and demand that my clients live up to them. I wouldn't be in their lives if they weren't looking to do something extraordinary. I work with people who are driven to do and become something big. We may not always know what it is in the beginning, but it's always transformational. Removing doubt, worry, pessimistic thoughts, and negative self talk is a *giant* part of the journey.

I worked with a thirty-eight-year-old man named Eric who was recovering from a heart attack. When I asked him what brought on the attack, he said he was stressed out all the time. He was in high-pressure sales and was very successful. The more we talked, the more I could tell that he had a knack for turning his worry into a story that supported it. But it kept him up at night, so, on top of the endless mind chatter, he was sleep deprived. No wonder this guy's heart gave out. When I asked Eric specifically what he worried about, he said, "Everything." That's a lot of worry!

"Give me an example," I said. I was curious where his first thoughts would go.

"I'm worried I might have another heart attack. If I do, what will happen to my kids? And what if I can't make a living and can't care for them?" He took me down a black diamond ski run of "what if's."

As I continued talking with Eric, I gave him an assignment. I wanted him to make a list of everything he worried about and then delegate all of his worries to me by emailing me his list. When I opened the document a few days later, it was *four* pages long. I'll give Eric credit for being thorough, but the list was full of empty concerns. I called him the next day to walk him through the list, one concern at a time, to ask the likelihood of them ever happening. As we clicked through the list, I asked, "Do you really think this will happen?"

"Probably not," he said.

"Then why are you giving it any space in your consciousness?"

In the end, only a handful of made-up worries were valid and worth his time and energy.

Most people are like Eric. They get stuck "what-iffing" themselves to death and spend all their time avoiding an issue by creating scenarios that may or may not exist.

"What if this happens?"

"What if I leave my relationship?"

"What if I quit my job?"

"What if I lose my job?"

You could play the "what-if" game for the rest of your life and you'd still be in the same place you started from. I call going down this worry route OMGWI—*oh my God what if*?

OMGWI is what stops us from living an extraordinary life. It kills people's dreams. It takes only two or three moves from an original thought to stop you cold. That's when you have to end the cycle by telling yourself "STOP!" When I find myself saying OMGWI, I say "STOP" out loud, even if I am by myself. The effect of doing this cancels the negative thought and brings me back to neutral.

I've walked into seminars where there are forty people and a thousand empty seats and think, What if no one else shows up? What if my marketing partners are upset? Then I quickly bring my thoughts right back around so I won't let my mind create a worst-case scenario.

Could my ego be bruised by lack of interest in Tom Ferry?

Hell, yes.

Will I die over it?

No.

Can I get over it and just focus on the people who are here?

Yup.

I remind myself that I am committed to helping people, even if it is forty at a time. In that case, I choose to give the best seminar ever and leave those people blown away by the experience.

> Being overwhelmed is in your head and is actually you being underplanned.

So, what do you really gain from worry? Worry is a mechanism that usually shuts people down. If that happens, you have plenty of time to swirl those negative thoughts around in your head and say things like, "I can't go to the gym," "I can't connect with my kid," "I can't get projects done on time," and "I'm so overwhelmed." What you don't understand is that worry is what's really bogging you down. Being consumed with worry means missing out on doing meaningful and important things in your life. Why should you go to the gym and work out, and still feel awful about the way you look, when you can just sit around and cry about it? Here's a what if: What if everything suddenly worked out for you? What would you do with all of that empty space in your head that used to be filled with doubt, fear, and worry?

Knowing what you now know about worry, how do you think it is impacting your life? What else could you be doing with the time you now spend worrying? What will you commit to right now to break the cycle of worry?

This chapter is one of the most important in my book because if you were to take away only one message from me it should be this: I want you to free yourself from the four addictions. If you do this, your life will become instantly and infinitely better.

I often wonder what my answer would be if someone asked me, as I asked Bill Mitchell, "What is the most important lesson you'd like to pass on?" What message would I want to leave behind as my legacy for my two sons, and what would I want them to understand about life so I could rest easy, knowing they would be well equipped, adjusted, and prepared for their future?"

In a perfect world, I would raise two great boys into men who would be free of the four addictions and would go out into the world and do big things for themselves, their families, and others. They would be able to follow their dreams, live their visions, and go for whatever they wanted to achieve regardless of what anybody else thought. They would be free of the past and they'd have the courage and self-esteem to move forward in spite of any mistakes they made along the way, because mistakes are experiences we can all learn from.

Thankfully, my kids get my message frequently and repeatedly. Occasionally, it's their old man who needs a tap on the shoulder to remind me that I sometimes fall victim to these addictions. My older son, Michael, is a terrific kid who loves sports and tries extremely hard when he's playing, especially basketball. I found myself watching a game last season worried that the game would be over before Michael got another chance to play. The clock was running down, his team was trailing by several points, and Michael was begging his coach to let him get back into the game. The coach put him in seconds before the final buzzer. As the clock ticked down, one of his teammates threw him the ball. It was a win the game/lose the game shot. Michael tossed the ball up, but it hit the rim and bounced out.

My heart immediately sank, and I worried that my boy would feel awful about losing the game (addiction to worry).

I wondered if other parents would be upset that Michael didn't make the winning shot (addiction to opinions of others).

All of these negative thoughts raced through my mind as I watched my son congratulate the other team (addiction to drama).

When he was through, Michael ran off the court happy as a clam. All he had wanted to do was play the game. I suddenly realized I had fallen into that addictive way of thinking and quickly reminded myself that it was a basketball game where nine-year-olds were out there doing their best. If other parents put any significance on that final shot, they had their own issues to deal with. I told Michael how proud I was and then took him out for a father son dinner.

I don't claim to be perfect. I am human, and even though I live By Design 99 percent of the time, things happen every day that test me. These are important moments to acknowledge because they keep me grounded, rooted in reality, and able to understand that we *all* can fall victim to these addictions. The key to creating long-lasting change in your life starts with acknowledging that you suffer from these addictions but are no longer willing to have them control your life.

CHAPTER

6

TURN AND FACE
THE CH-CH-CHANGES

By now you've read enough to know that you're most likely living by default. If I've done my job right so far, you're eager and motivated to begin your shift toward living By Design. I've made you aware of any resistance in your life, so the only thing that will stop you from transitioning from by default to By Design is your choice not to proceed, which stems from your fear of change.

Change is a sudden disruption in the way you've been living that forces you to see the world from a new perspective. Change is often uncomfortable. But know this: You are driving the train that is pulling your professional and personal well-being. Your angst is a sign you're on the right track.

Change can occur in several ways. It can be brought on by a crisis, such as losing your job or being diagnosed with a debilitating disease. It can occur cyclically, when things simply change around you, such as a child going off to college or your own retirement. And there is visionary change, which I focus on in this chapter. Visionary change is the most empowering kind of change because it inspires and requires you to be proactive in your own life.

Do you have the strength, the desire, and the *courage* to make that shift—to change?

Courage is the ability to face danger, difficulty, uncertainty, or pain without being overcome by fear or being deflected from a chosen course of action. It is a willingness to look fear in the eye, accept the worst-case scenario, and continue to take action anyway.

Mark Twain said, "Courage is the mastery of fear—not the absence of it." I say that courage is the power to act in spite of fear. General George Patton, one of America's greatest military leaders, admitted that he was "not a brave man" but "an utter craven coward." He said the sound of gunshots or the sight of battle made his hands sweat from being scared. What he mastered was how to gain power over his fears and not continue to let them control him.

To me, courage is 10 percent fear, 30 percent imagination, 30 percent preparation, and 30 percent faith. Without courage, there is only fear, hesitancy, complacency, and lack of action. All of these traits are the kiss of death when your goal is living an extraordinary life.

Many of my clients work in the real estate and financial business. Courage and fear are an often-talked-about subject because, like most of us, my clients live in a "wait and see" marketplace. I don't believe in wait and see. I believe in "think, create, and then do!" I often call myself a calculated risk taker. I tell clients to go out and take some action every day, even if it's small, because no one knows what will happen next. If you have a wait-and-see mind-set, you'll never discover what's around the corner. Before you know it, time, opportunity, and life will pass you by. Remember, a *bend* in the road is not the *end* of the road.

Human beings have an unbelievable obsession with fixing things, yet uncertainty is one thing that can't be fixed. It just is. Learn to find peace in the unknown.

There are numerous ways to motivate people, but there is only one way I know to *keep* people motivated, and that is for them to be *self-motivated*. Here's what I mean. All external motivation is temporary. Many people read something or go to a seminar that temporarily fires them up and readies them to make a change. Unfortunately, most of those people end up doing nothing. Lasting motivation, a motive to act, comes from inspiration. My definition of inspiration is being imbued with the spirit to act. Motivation without inspiration doesn't last. What happens when you lose your motivation? You return to old habits and your same old comfortable behavior—and remain living by default.

Most people stay in their comfortable, complacent place because they aren't willing to go through the pain that usually comes with change. Leaving a stale relationship, choosing to switch careers, or taking control of one's health or finances are painful situations that people avoid until something happens and they have to deal with them. And it's not always pain that people fear. Indecision, rejection, or an unwillingness to accept the worst-case scenario can also hold them back.

Courage is having the ability to decide what you really want and then going after it despite the pain. It's having the fortitude to choose a direction and then take the necessary action. My good friend, mentor, and bestselling author Brian Tracy once told me that

I had to be comfortable with running all my ideas up the flagpole. If it works, he said, keep them up there. If it doesn't work, bring them back down and send up other flags until you find some that do work. Obviously this means you have to be willing to discover things through trial and error. To live By Design, you must be willing to take action, make mistakes, live through the pain, and have faith in your decisions.

Faith and fear have similar definitions—a belief in the unknown. If I am fearful, I believe in the unknown just as I do when I have faith. Being present in uncertainty gives you an edge that other people lack. Practicing this means you can't just think outside the box anymore. You have to think inside it and around it, and kick it, shake it, and do whatever it takes to get through your hard times.

So, are you ready to get inspired, take action, make some mistakes, live through pain and upset, have faith in your decisions, and then trust in them? If you're willing, I will give you the tools and the courage to move forward with fearless faith to transition—By Design.

I saw a story on ESPN a few years ago about a young man born with cerebral palsy. Doctors told Ben Comen he'd probably never walk, let alone run. Even though walking was painful and awkward for Ben, he had a lifelong dream to be on a team with other kids. He wanted to fit in and be one of the guys. Over the years, coaches allowed Ben to be on a team, but they never let him compete. He sat on the sidelines and participated by offering his teammates water as they finished their events. He could cheer for his team, but he always dreamed that he'd someday hear the sound of his team cheering *him* on. His dream came true the day his coach in junior high school gave him a chance to belong. He did what any great coach would do—he told Ben and his parents he'd figure out something so Ben could compete.

Miraculously, Ben ran cross-country races throughout the rest of his school years. He never competed against anyone but himself. It sometimes took Ben forty minutes to do what the other kids did in fifteen, but he did it anyway. That's courage. When Ben sometimes fell during a race, he picked himself up and kept right on running.

I was so moved by Ben's heroic story that I asked him to speak at one of my seminars a few years ago. I shared his story with my clients and then brought him onto the stage, where he was met by a standing ovation from the crowd of 2,500 clients. I asked Ben to share his thoughts on inspiration, where to find courage, and how to succeed against all odds.

"What's it like when you fall down?" I asked.

Ben said, "I just know our bodies are designed to get up and keep moving forward. We're not meant to fall down and stay there. We're meant to get up and keep fighting the fight. I tell myself, 'It's just a fall. Get up and keep going.' "

I was awed by Ben's wisdom and freedom. His body is racked with pain. It is agony for this young man to do what most of us take for granted, and yet he endures his pain so he can live his life with passion.

Fear never goes away, so you may as well learn to say, "Hello, fear, I see you but I'm going to do this anyway!"

Look, we all have a dragon that needs slaying. There is always something we will have to conquer in our lives—whether it's cleaning up an old relationship, making a current relationship work, getting into better physical condition, or earning the money we want or adjusting our lifestyle to live with less.

So when you get down to it, what really holds you back and keeps you living by default is a combination of fear, the four addictions, and complacency. These have allowed you to accept a mediocre life as *enough*. Most people won't take action to break away from those comfortable traits to risk having an extraordinary life.

Something else keeps you living by default, and this time it isn't you. It's the enabler in your life who gains a direct benefit by allowing or being part of your default world. An enabler empowers another person to do something. Often, these relationships are considered to be codependent. To be fair, some enablers inspire us to do good things. However, others promote negative, sometimes harmful behavior. And although life often provides each of us with countless opportunities to be one or the other, I address only enablers who hold us back, cover up for our mistakes, and empower us to pursue a life not just of wrongdoing (with drugs or alcohol, abusive behavior, dishonesty, and more) but by enabling us to be lethargic, making the wrong food choices, not addressing our financial issues, or resisting healthy relationships. I also refer to enablers who feed the four primary addictions discussed in Chapter Five.

> Sharon Wegscheider-Cruse, in her work as a well-respected family therapist, suggests that 96 percent of the general population exhibits some forms of codependent (enabling) behavior at one time or another or in a fairly consistent pattern or both.

We've all been in a place where someone close to us was going through a rough time, perhaps finding out that a best friend was having an affair, or seeing a co-worker fall behind at the office or participate in self-destructive behavior, creating problems for our friend such as drug abuse or an abusive home situation. If you're like most people, you've probably kept your mouth shut and stepped away from the situation to avoid becoming part of the drama. If that's what you've done, you've been an enabler. We've all been there, and we all have enablers in our lives.

Enablers like or are willing to accept things as they are. They're comfortable with the status quo. They've been there before and know how to keep you mired in your addictions. If you want to break free from living by default, you have to recognize the enablers in your life; they are more than likely part of the problem. Or *you* may be the enabler in someone else's life.

Most research talks about the characteristics of an enabler as it pertains to substance abuse or addiction, but several of those traits carry over to what keeps you living by default. Common to all enablers is any behavior that violates your internal value system, resulting in feelings of guilt, remorse, and self-loathing, and then is justified with rationalizations. Statements such as, "Last night wasn't that bad," "I've seen Jack angrier than that before," and "If you were in my shoes, you'd understand why I do what I do" are all projected causes that an individual believes to be true. Enablers want to shield or protect themselves from their own circumstances. Unfortunately, their well-intentioned or self-protective behavior plays a large role in keeping both people stuck in their destructive behaviors. Continual use of these rationalizations results in both people losing touch with reality. So, what really happens is that both people brand their own reality, which becomes comfortable, easier than dealing with the truth, and habitual. It's their routine, the story they tell themselves.

We all know couples who thrive on drama, right? The wife is always fifteen minutes late and the husband is angry about it every time. Monday you're employed and by Friday you're not. You make love to your spouse on Saturday night thinking that life has never been better together, and on Sunday morning she tells you she wants a divorce.

Truth is circumstantial. What is true on Monday may not be true on Friday. The goal is to live in your truth every day. If both people keep the codependent relationship as is, they end up supporting each other's misunderstanding of the true nature of their problems. The result is that they are both engaged in a successful self-deception that allows the issues to remain hidden, and they continue as they always have.

Whether you are the enabler or the one being enabled, the best way to stop the detrimental cycle is to become aware of its existence.

SURE SIGNS OF ENABLING BEHAVIORS

- You find yourself worrying that someone cannot handle a situation without you.
- You are consumed with other people's lives.
- You excuse or rationalize someone's unacceptable behavior.
- You want to reduce someone's discomfort by constantly providing for them.
- You are overprotective.
- You feel responsible for everyone else.
- You feel manipulated but do nothing to change your circumstances.
- You believe you are the only person who understands him/her.
- You always make yourself available on a moment's notice, even when you don't have time.
- You see characteristics of yourself in him/her.

If you're an enabler, you must take responsibility for being part of the cause and effect.

Several years ago I decided that people who wanted me to lie for them were not people I wanted in my life. I would only be enabling or reinforcing their bad behavior, which I had no interest in doing. A buddy asked me to lie about extramarital affairs he was having. He'd call me up and say, "If my wife asks you where we were yesterday, just tell her we were in a meeting all day."

Every time he called, I explained that his request made me very uncomfortable and my MO wasn't to perpetuate lies for anyone. If I complied with his requests, his affairs would become part of my life, inviting unnecessary drama and aggravation that I simply didn't want or need to take on. Further, doing so would make me an enabler, someone who contributed to his bad behavior. I make a living helping people break those cycles, not continue them. When I expressed how I felt, he interpreted me as being confrontational. But I stood firm because I didn't want to participate in covering up for him. I want to believe he respected me for my conviction. I don't think his intention was to turn me into a liar, but I could have been seen that way if I chose to appease him.

If you strive to live By Design, one of your biggest jobs is to spend as much time as you can intentionally feeling good. You must do everything in your power, every day, to control how you feel, which means speaking up when something makes you uncomfortable. If you don't practice this daily, you will inevitably keep living by default.

A man I know about wakes up every morning thinking the same thing—he hates his life. He's fifty years old and recently divorced for the second time, and he feels emotionally disconnected from his children. He has several acquaintances but few friends and feels alone all the time. He thinks of his job as a necessary evil, believes that his position isn't secure, and wants to quit, especially before the "man" can

You can be both an addict and an enabler. Which, if not both, are you?

get him. He has very little money in the bank and thinks retirement anytime soon is impossible. He's overweight and on medication to feel good but never does. He finds himself repeating the same questions over and over:

"How did I get to this point?"

"Why does this keep happening to me?"

"Is this all there is to life?"

"Will things ever get better?"

"Why me?"

I know a woman, also fifty years old, who is in a healthy, loving marriage, is close to her children, has an active social life and many close friends, and is passionate about her work. She feels fulfilled in accomplishing everyday tasks, is physically fit, and enjoys exercising. She has invested her money wisely, is happy with her life, has many hobbies, and includes charitable goals in her early retirement.

What if I told you they were siblings, grew up in the same household, went to the same schools, had the same relationship with their parents, went to the same church, traveled on the same family vacations, graduated from the same college with the same degree, and even worked for the same company?

Why is one so miserable, questioning his past, present, and future, struggling through life, career, relationships, health, finances, and family, while the other is enormously happy, feeling joy and gratitude for her life?

One had the courage to live By Design, to step up and try something different—to say, "Against all odds I will make it"—while the other lived by default, allowing the circumstances of his life to decide his fate. They were handed the same deck of cards, and each decided how to play them.

It's as if a wall had been placed in the middle of the path of their life journey. Each sibling had to make a choice. So, too, here you are. You've come to a fork in the road. You cannot go straight, so you must choose a direction—By Design or by default?

PHASE

II

LIVING BY DESIGN

CHAPTER

6 STEPS TO LIVING BY DESIGN

Phase I of this book focuses on helping you define, discover, and become aware of all the areas in your life that you are living by default. It is important to reread the first phase and identify your areas of default so you can smoothly ease into Phase II, Living By Design. It's crucial to have a clear idea of all the areas you want to address in this next section of the book so you can get the most out of it.

I am excited that you've come this far and are willing to take the next steps to create positive change for yourself. If living by default is a failure to decide how you want your life to be or settling for the circumstances of your situation, living By Design is living with clarity, inspiration, and power, free of resistance, determined to do whatever it takes to be your best. It's your path toward creating a vision that inspires you by setting goals, creating a plan, and then taking massive action to achieve anything you want. It's choosing to be responsible and the victor rather than the victim of the circumstances of your life.

Living By Design is the willingness to have things fall apart, knowing you can endure the short-term pain to find the opportunities that exist on the other side. You will make difficult choices along the way, but remember this: They are short term. I have always believed that the bigger the break*down,* the bigger the opportunity for a break*through.* Things fall apart so they can fall together.

My clients love simple formulas. They want answers and long-lasting results. So, check this out. The basic principle behind living By Design is:

the right attitude + the right action + the right structure = an extraordinary life!

Easy enough, right? Well, if it were really easy, everyone would be doing it. How many people do you know who practice this? I suspect not many. The good news is you are well on your way to becoming one of them.

Are you ready?

If feelings determine your attitude, then your attitude determines the actions you take, or don't take—which, by the way, is also an action. It's the choice to do nothing at all. Your actions determine the kind of life you live. This process is a continuous circle. It's a cycle that works both By Design and by default. But from this point forward, I focus on helping you make the transition to By Design.

Living By Design can be achieved through the six-step plan I developed to help my clients live an extraordinary life. Its universal appeal and success, based on its incredible and rapid results, have helped tens of thousands of people make a positive shift in their lives. And although I know you'll be thrilled with the constructive changes you'll see in your own life, the plan does require commitment, discipline, and a willingness to change. Let me be perfectly candid: It's not easy and it takes hard work, dedication, and perseverance. But if you're willing to power through to the next level in your life, I promise that the results will astound you.

The first three steps were created to help you plan what you want. The next three steps are ways to attract what you want into your life. Although it may seem selfish at first to say, "I'm choosing to have my life be this way," achieving your vision will benefit everyone around you. It will be like tossing a pebble into a lake, creating a ripple of positive benefits for everyone. Put aside your doubt, your cynicism that you've read books like this before and nothing changed. Let go of all your negativity and become open to the possibilities. Are you ready to get started?

Step 1: Wake up from your coma—become aware of the areas in your life that need attention.

Step 1 is as simple as saying, "Hello, my name is (your name here) and I have been living by default." As discussed in Phase I, becoming aware is all about discovering the things that make you feel uncomfortable and addressing them. It's time to wake up and realize that your past actions are what put you in your self-induced coma in the first place. Those actions have taken away your power and put you into a victim mind-set, where you feel as if you have absolutely no control over your life. When you wake up from your coma, you will begin to regain that control.

When I ask clients to write down their three main goals, without fail they respond with wanting to improve their relationships, health, and finances. I discovered a long time ago that most people won't address the other issues in their life if their finances aren't satisfactory. Financial stress is the number one cause of relationship failure. When you're making money, you feel good and you're creative, expressive, and open. When your actions are inspired, you're making a difference in the world. When you're making a difference, you make more money. It's a positive cycle that epitomizes living By Design.

Conversely, when you're not making money, all of those inspired actions tend to dry up. You get stuck, become frozen with fear, and resist change. This is a perfect example of how one core area being in default can negatively affect all the others. Although most people start with the first three categories—career, intimate relationships, and finances—I always try to reiterate that the remaining four—physical health, spirituality, contribution/giving back, and desire to learn and grow—are equally important to creating a strong balance and quality of life.

If your intention in buying this book is to make more money or have a better relationship, that would be easy to accomplish. What I'm talking about here is having it all. You might be doing well at work, but everything else is death in your wake. Is one area of success enough? Wealth isn't about how much money you make. Focusing on wealth alone is a limited perspective. To me, true wealth is defined by our relationships with one another, with ourselves, and with some higher guide. It is found in the quality of our love life, our social life, our philanthropic endeavors, and our career. If you are in search of true wealth, then you are, without a doubt, seeking a life By Design.

The Core Value Assessment was created to help you set forth specific intentions of what you want out of life as well as why you want it. Depending on your answers, you may need to address all or some of the Core Seven, which includes your career, intimate relationships, finances, physical health, spirituality, contribution/giving back, and desire to learn and grow. I suggest starting with the areas you think need the most attention. If your career is mostly on track but your relationships are not, focus on creating a plan to improve your relationships. If your finances are in trouble, there's an urgency to create a plan to get them back on track. It's important to know which areas need your focus so you can make immediate changes and start seeing positive results.

If you didn't answer the questions in the Core Value Assessment on page 56, do so now. You cannot move on with the following steps to live By Design without going through that process first. Failure to do so will keep you living by default, and our work here will be done. If you did answer those questions earlier, bravo, my friend. You are clearly committed to your desire to live By Design.

If you are still uncertain about your ability to accurately and honestly assess your life, ask someone close to you for help. But choose that person wisely because you are now in an exposed place and this process will make you feel vulnerable. You cannot be the hardened warrior who has no problems and no issues and is coming into this merely to feed your ego. The By Design plan is predicated on honesty and your ability to see things as they really are.

When you face your answers, you may feel a little resistance or pain because you've engaged your senses and emotions. I want you to *feel* something when you think about the Core Seven categories and the answers you gave for each.

Is there room for something more?

Do you want to improve in these areas?

If you have a satisfying job or a successful business, how are your relationships?

Are you as connected as you could be to your spouse/partner?

Do you feel good about your kids and their futures?

How do you feel about your friendships?

Do you feel good standing naked in front of the mirror?
Are you satisfied with your income, savings, and investments?
Do you take care of everyone else, leaving nothing left for you?
Do you contribute enough to others, or is it all about you right
   now?
Are you spiritually in a good place?

Ask yourself *enough* questions and the *right* questions to feel pain and discomfort. Don't be afraid to delve into the dark places you've kept hidden away all these years. Bring the family secrets to the surface and allow your emotions to bubble over.

Show me a flawless person and I'll show you someone who has learned to cover up their deep wounds. We all have pain, my friend. I have pain just as you do. Look, when you get sick, sometimes the doctor prescribes rest to get better, while other times it takes something more. The same holds true when you self-assess. Sometimes you can ask surface questions that will evoke emotional responses, and other times you've got to go deeper, all the way into your heart and soul.

Some people reading this book will understand Step 1 and be able to complete it on their own. Others may need to take this action one step further, and to give their answers to someone they trust and say, "This is what I think. What do *you* think?"

Here's a tip when asking for someone else's opinion on something this personal: Tell them they've got your permission to speak as freely as possible because you are really committed to change. Let them know you want them to be authentic in their response. Create a safe environment so they know they can be completely honest and you will not become defensive. Agree that you will listen without fear or judgment and then allow them to speak without being interrupted.

My mentor and good friend Bill Mitchell once told me, "No true relationship can exist where the fear of the consequences of the truth are present." You're in this to win. You're reading this book and you've come this far because you want an extraordinary life, don't you?

> "No true relationship can exist where the fear of the consequences of the truth are present."
>
> —Bill Mitchell

Step 2: Make the choice to change your life.

Knowing you are in need of life adjustments is a great start, but it simply isn't enough. You have to *act* on it. The more pain you can associate with the way you no longer want to be, the more likely you are to make the necessary changes. Don't be afraid to get upset or a little depressed or to have regret for letting the pendulum swing so far out of bounds. Those emotions are what will drive your declaration that you've made the right decision and that it is time to change.

Change is hard, not only for you but for everyone around you. Your family and friends may have a more difficult time with your desire to change because they live so comfortably in your default world. I call these people "defaulters." They're the ones who worry about what your changes will mean for *them*. In some cases, they may not be part of your future plans because they simply don't fit into the new vision. For example, if you've been living with your partner in a passionless relationship and your goal is to have a relationship full of passion, which you know your partner isn't capable of giving to you, you will likely be faced with making a hard decision to leave that relationship.

Let's look at that particular circumstance. Is the decision hard for *you*? Or does it merely *appear* hard because of the effect it will have on someone else? More important, is the relationship one of mutual default or mutual design?

By default would be choosing to stay in the relationship and allow things to remain exactly the same because it is easier than making changes or leaving. By Design is the willingness to confront the situation, create mutual solutions, and try to fix the problem. If, after attempts to improve your relationship, you both feel you gave it your best effort but still can't come to a place of mutual satisfaction, By Design would be making the choice to leave so you both can have what you want.

Let's say you're living with a man who is eating himself toward a heart attack, and you want to take control of your health and vitality. You've made a commitment to eating healthier, exercising more, and not overindulging.

How does his behavior impact yours?

Do you eat a little more than you should or make the wrong food choices when you're together?

How do you think those habits affect other areas of your life?

Do they affect your sleep patterns?

Exercise routine?

Are you gaining weight and feeling tired all the time?

And, if you're overeating, are you living as a positive example for your children?

A classic example of this dilemma is when a husband gains weight during his wife's pregnancy. The idea is that you'll both go through pregnancy, both gain the baby weight, and then lose it together after the baby is born. More often than not, the baby comes, but the excess weight never goes.

Why?

Because you've both fallen into unhealthy habits that can seem impossible to break.

But what happens when only one of you decides to change?

That would probably rock your partner's world to the core, especially if you've become so codependent on each other that you've learned to justify the results of overindulging and overeating, and a lethargic lifestyle.

Now you're faced with a real dilemma. Do you begin to change your habits so you can get healthy, improve your appearance, and understand how lousy you were feeling by discovering what feeling "good" really is? Or do you choose to continue those habits by convincing yourself that things aren't so bad?

It seems like a no-brainer to me, yet many people stay right where they are—in their comfort zone of mediocrity.

Why?

They're still living by default.

Living By Design sometimes requires making painful choices that are good for you. In many cases those choices will ultimately be good for everyone involved, even if that is hard to see in the moment. Pain is a natural part of change. We've all heard the saying "No pain, no gain" when we're working out, but that philosophy holds true outside the gym too, especially when it comes to personal growth. Thankfully, we are wired to eventually forget that pain so we can heal and move on. Even so, we have to live through the pain to realize the gain.

The following exercise will help drive you to create your clearest vision for what you want to achieve. If you choose *not* to change your default way of living, make sure you write down the negative consequences of your conscious behavior, as hard as that may be. You will feel naked, as if you ripped off all your clothes and ran around your favorite restaurant. But here's the deal. You cannot pass go, and will not collect two hundred dollars, without doing this exercise.

You must get present to the negative consequences of not changing as well as with the positive benefits of living By Design. One of those lists of consequences will emotionally drive you to make a change or not. We live in a yin/yang world, which means that this exercise should give you both pleasure and pain. You cannot create a

EXERCISE

1. Write out as many emotional benefits of choosing to live By Design as you can think of. For example, the benefits of living By Design in your relationships might include having a healthier, more loving and nurturing connection with your partner that gives you a true feeling of warmth, stability, security, joy, passion, sex, and anything else you want in your relationship that is not currently satisfying. Another example is the benefits of By Design living for your health, which may include living longer, having better flexibility, being more energetic and less tired, and feeling good about the way you look.

   So, what are all of the positive benefits you will experience from living By Design? Write your answers below.

   _____

   _____

   _____

   _____

   _____

   _____

2. What are the consequences of staying by default? Perhaps you will continue to financially spiral downward because you have no inspiration or plan, which means you will never earn enough money, you will always have the stress of being behind on payments, your debts will dominate your thoughts every night,

you'll suffer through every holiday, and you will feel like a loser every time children say, "can I have . . . ," knowing they cannot because you never made the choice to change. The more painful this exercise, the better. The more painful the consequences, the more real you are being with yourself. If you wrote it down, you know there's a possibility of its happening if you don't make the change. I dare you to list ten of the most real, painful, gut-wrenching realities of staying on the course of living by default in any of the Core Seven categories of your life.

Write your answers below:

_____

_____

_____

_____

_____

vision for your life By Design without being present to both so you can become aware of your real motivation.

Will you be driven by the benefits of your decision or by the negative consequences of changing? I want you to be present with and driven by *all* possibilities. Are you more inclined to move away from the negative consequences or toward them because you're comfortable there?

Don't worry about which list drives you. Embrace it. Some of the most successful people I know are driven by their fear and the possible pain they'll feel if they don't get up every morning and do all the things they're supposed to do to be extraordinary. It's not that they live their life with a consciousness of that pain. They have an acute awareness that this is how they're wired so they use it to their advantage.

Knowing what you now know about living by default, it is completely irresponsible to continue living that way. You are allowing your circumstances to dictate how you're going to operate. That doesn't work for me, and I know it isn't working for you. Once you have identified the consequences of living by default, I'm afraid there's no turning back because now you know that these consequences are worth changing for. If you do fall back into negligent ways, you now have the knowledge and awareness that you've got no one to blame but yourself.

It's all about you, friend. No one else is playing puppet master with your life. When you choose to change your ways, *you* become the puppet master, the one pulling the strings, controlling your every movement with precision and ease. You will dictate the outcome of everything you do and understand that the universe is unfolding exactly as it should.

Step 3: Create your life By Design.

Now that you have an awareness of the resistance and the issues in your life and are present with your motivation to change, you can move on to Step 3, which is about getting clear on what you really want for yourself in each category. It's a time to create new intentions, gain clarity, and see yourself the way you want to be. Let's call your new intentions your *vision* for life By Design. This is one of the hardest steps because it's now 100 percent you who controls the outcome.

To help you envision your path, you must first declare what you want. This is the step where the four addictions really show up and is where most people get stuck. You will definitely wrestle with some of your demons. Don't get caught up in the drama or old stories you've told yourself over the years; simply acknowledge them for what they are—boulders in your river. For a moment, instead of reverting to the past, wondering or worrying about what anyone else will think, allow yourself to dream. If you could become present with how great your life could be, what would your life look like?

I ask you to answer several thought-provoking, life-changing questions. These are the same questions I asked myself when I was vacillating about leaving our family business to start my own. My coach at the time, Mike Vance, who mentored and coached many important executives over the years and was referred to by Walt Disney as the most creative man in North America, asked me these same questions when I was mapping out my own future. They literally changed and thereby saved my life.

Be forewarned: Answering these questions can set you on a path you never saw coming—whether it's starting your own business or ending up at an ashram in India trying to solve issues of world hunger. When you live By Design, you live with passion and purpose; therefore, *anything* is possible. Answer these questions as authentically as you can. Don't edit yourself or hold back. Trust your gut. You're having those thoughts for a reason.

- Why are you here and what's your purpose?
- How do you want to come across to others; what are your values?
- What are your God-given talents?
- Five years from now, how will the world experience you?
- Who would you be if you were already there?

And because you've gone this far, you can now appreciate the following bonus question I've added to Mike's original set.

- What do you need to let go of to take the next step?

These important yet difficult questions are the key to unlocking your future and the path that will lead you to live By Design. So they shouldn't be rushed through or undertaken lightly. You should approach them as if making a life-changing decision. That is exactly what the questions are designed for.

When you are living By Design, you will find yourself repeatedly coming back to these six questions. Therefore, I suggest getting a notebook or journal you can freely write in whenever you face answering these questions. One of the benefits of keeping your answers is that you can revisit your thoughts and vision, which will help you tweak it as you progress.

A popular book was written a few years ago called *The Secret* that basically tells readers they have the power to attract anything and manifest everything they want in life by simply asking for it. Think about that . . . by just "asking for it." When the book was published, I explored the subject in my seminars. I asked my audiences how many of them had read the book. Almost every hand shot up. Next I asked, "And how many of you are practicing the principles you learned?" Again, almost every hand was raised. Finally I asked, "How many of you are getting everything you want?" A couple of hands went up. The rest of the audience looked a little ashamed.

I paused, crouched down, cupped my hands around the corners of my mouth, and said, "Do you want to know the *real* secret?"

The entire audience shouted, "YES!"

"Okay, here's the deal. The real secret is that you have to know what you want, know why you want it, and then work your ass off every single day to get it!"

The audience nodded in agreement to my message. After all, sitting around hoping you'll manifest a Ferrari doesn't work. I went on to explain that all of us have to fight through our fears and then take *action* if we want such luxuries. Live as the person we want to be; and when we start to get close to what we want, we must push a little harder to actually get it. Be grateful for what you have, and then be in massive action—always working, always advancing toward your goals, until you achieve what you want. It's not just *asking* for it; you've got to actually *do the work*!

> Be conscious and aware that the four addictions will rear their heads right about now. Don't get caught up in your worry or drama or the idea that you may have tried but failed in the past or what other people will say or think. Keep pushing through.

The Greek philosopher Aristotle said that the formula for happiness and success was to first have a definite, clear, practical idea, goal, or objective. Second, attain it by whatever means available, whether wisdom, money, materials, or methods. Third, adjust all your means to that end.

A lot of people get caught between the creation of their vision and their intention of their goal, by getting stuck in the "how."

Do you want to know what I have to say to that?

Phucow!

It's a made-up word that means, "Stop worrying about *how* you're going to do it and just do it!" Get clear on what you want, and the "how" will reveal itself. "How" is the easy part of living By Design. Once you become present with what you want, the social proof, natural pathways, meetings, information, strategies, and data points will show up everywhere if you're paying attention.

Every three weeks or so I have an appointment to have my hair cut by my friend Daniel, a guy I refer to as my "hairapist." We spend most of my time in the chair talking about life, family, hopes, goals, and dreams. One day, Daniel told me that his true passion was creating art, but his hours at the salon wouldn't allow him enough time to pursue both careers. He said he was stuck cutting hair from ten in the morning until eight o'clock at night five or six days a week, leaving him little time for anything else.

I asked him what would happen if he shifted his hours to be in the salon from five or six in the morning until two o'clock in the afternoon. If he was able to do that, would he still have enough time, energy, and stamina to do his art?

"Tom, I can't cut hair at five o'clock in the morning!" Daniel protested.

I immediately reassured him that I would be his first client if he changed his hours. I was certain that all of the busy executives he worked with would appreciate the shift in schedule so they no longer had to take valuable working hours from their day to get a haircut.

In that one moment, we shifted Daniel's entire business. Several months later, he said that our conversation changed his life because he realized he was getting stuck in the "how" instead of zeroing in on the target. That was the day that he and I coined the word "phucow!"

By being open to the "how" (changing his schedule) and asking his clients if they would meet him earlier, he no longer had an excuse to not be doing the art he was so passionate about. Daniel was able to generate over six figures in sales from his art in eighteen months while continuing to maintain his existing business as a stylist. To this day, I am his steady once-a-month 6 a.m. appointment.

Focus on what you want, create your vision, and allow the "how" to show up. After twenty years of living By Design, I know I am not the first to say that if you can find a model or a mentor, someone who has already successfully done what you are desiring, this will allow you to leapfrog past unnecessary obstacles or struggles. When I set forth my intention to write this book and inspire a million people to live and work By Design, I had already written a book on my own, but it was industry driven and self-published and used as a calling card to help build my business in the early days. I knew that if I wanted to achieve my vision, I would have to seek out and learn from people who had already done what I intended to do.

So, how did I accomplish this?

I picked up the phone and reached out to two people who I knew had achieved what I wanted. The first was T. Harv Eker, author of *Secrets of the Millionaire Mind*. After numerous calls and a fierce game of phone tag, we connected. Within an hour, he revealed so many insights, ahas, do's and don'ts, pitfalls to avoid, and specific marketing strategies that my vision became even more real. I am forever indebted to Harv for paying it forward by sharing his insights so openly.

My second call was to someone I have been blessed to know for close to two decades, the incredible Mark Victor Hansen, co-author of the *Chicken Soup for the Soul* series and several other bestselling books. Once again, I was learning from someone who had been down this path numerous times. He shed light where there was none. His insights and experience were invaluable and helped me become present with significant milestones that were in alignment with my achieving my vision. Coming from a guy whose combined book sales are over 700 million copies, I can still see the smile on his face when he said, "Only a million copies, Tom? You're thinking too small!" (You see? Sometimes we all need a coach!)

After spending time with these two guys, I was able to map out the steps that would naturally and automatically lead me to accomplish a goal that, prior to those two phone calls, I was clueless about achieving. With their knowledge and guidance, I sat down and began creating my *vision board*.

I once read a statistic that at least 65 percent of all people are considered "visual," meaning that they best respond to visual stimulation. One way to see your vision come to life is by creating a vision board, a visual example of what you want your life to look like. A vision board is a map of your plan and the significant milestones on the way toward accomplishing your goal. It taps into the neuropsychology of self-discipline that says if you have a visual representation of how you're going to get there, you will clearly see the path to your goal.

I don't know about you, but I am the type of guy who likes to know exactly where I'm driving. It makes me uncomfortable when I don't have a GPS system or directions from MapQuest to get me from point A to point B. Think about a vision board as your personal GPS system that shows you each step you'll have to take to reach your destination.

I encourage using a vision board for each of the Core Seven areas of your life because it answers who you need to be, what steps you need to take to meet all of your goals, and what you need to create to have your vision show up in your world.

Specifically, a vision board can help you answer questions such as:

What would happen along the path toward meeting the man or woman of your dreams?

What milestones would occur along the way to achieving your ideal weight?

—to achieving your ideal professional position?

—to achieving the contribution you want to make to your community or charity?

—to completing a specific task, finishing a certification, or—what the heck—writing a bestselling book?

Mike Vance told me a story about Walt Disney and the legend of his secret wall. Allegedly, Disney used to hang up sketches and ideas he had for new companies, products, characters, and rides on a top-secret hidden wall in his office. It was a private place where the dreamer could dream. I think everyone should have a secret wall because it provides a place to display your dreams, regardless of how crazy or big they may be.

My secret wall is in my home office. I constantly display all the things I want to accomplish in a visual way that clearly states, This is my intention, this is where I'm going, and this is what I'm working on to make it happen. It's in my face every time I walk through the door. My vision board maps out the milestones, as I see them, unfolding in my mind from beginning to end. A vision board doesn't mean that all of these milestones will occur. It gives you an incentive to reach for each of them, but by no means should it be viewed as a failure if that doesn't happen—unless, of course, you failed to take the proper action, set it into motion, and do whatever it took to get you there.

My vision board for this book looked like this:

1. Assemble a great team.
2. Create the outline for the book.
3. Meet with publishers and sell the book.
4. Celebrate the signing of publishing contract.
5. Write the book.
6. Begin premarketing.
7. Successfully sell book in presales via the Internet and other channels.
8. Begin book tour and connecting with thousands of people inspired to live By Design.
9. Do publicity.
10. Celebrate making bestseller list with team.

Keep your vision board in your office, your bathroom, on a small piece of paper that you carry around with you, or wherever you will be inspired by the constant reminder of what you want and what you're committed to. As I meet my goals, I revisit my vision boards to make adjustments. I have one-, three-, and five-year goals that need to be tweaked from time to time. I assess each area of my life—where I'm at and what's going on—ask for feedback from my wife, and do all of these exercises to keep my vision boards fresh, current, and relevant.

To be clear, just because you found a great model and mapped out a vision board, it doesn't mean that the challenges, obstacles, and pitfalls won't show up. Think of your vision board like the board game Chutes and Ladders. Do you remember that game? The goal was a race from beginning to end. Sometimes when you rolled the dice, you landed on a ladder that propelled you forward, past several spots, toward the finish line. But there were also times when you landed on a chute or a slide, which set you back multiple spots and meant you had to climb back up to where you had been. Keep in mind that your vision board is just like Chutes and Ladders. Sometimes you will catch a break, and other times there will be setbacks. The key is not to give up, to learn from the lesson and then get back to work on your plan.

One last thought on vision boards: Don't be overly attached to hitting every milestone that you've set forth. Remember, you created this plan. Once in it, you may discover that some milestones you wrote down aren't necessary, and others you achieved didn't produce the results you desired. Feel comfortable knowing you can always add new milestones to your plan. And not hitting a milestone should not be viewed as a failure but rather a lesson learned.

One common mistake people make when they hear me talking about a vision board is to confuse it with a dream board. A dream board contains photos of things you *think* you want. It is made up of pictures cut out from magazines, catalogs, or books that represent everything you want—perhaps a fancy car, a beautiful home, a new watch, a healthy body, or even a happy, loving family on vacation together. Dream boards can be effective as temporary motivators. But though I don't discourage them, there's not a lot of purpose behind them unless you've got an overriding plan to turn those dreams into visions.

I once met a young man whom I called the "thirty-year-old virgin." I don't think he had ever been on a real date and yet he had five photos of recognizable supermodels on his dream board. When I asked him "why," he responded, "These are the kind of women I want to be with."

I couldn't blame the guy for dreaming big, but I also knew that it was not currently realistic for him to attract a woman like this.

I said, "Without a vision and a plan to accomplish this, having those photos on your dream board is a complete waste of time and space." I wasn't trying to burst his bubble so much as I was aiming to motivate him to create a realistic plan to achieve his goal.

Don't just tell me you want a brand-new Maserati, *show* me how you plan to own one. I don't know many people who have achieved all the things they've pasted on their dream board, but I do know a lot of people who have had a vision and a plan and worked to acquire those things as a result.

Whenever we take a vacation, I encourage my sons to make a list of all the things they'd like to do together as a family. One of the activities they had been begging for was learning to paddleboard because they watched guys doing it in the bay near our house. They were enchanted with the idea of getting up on a board. So the boys and I decided to take some lessons and learn to ride.

We pulled up to our favorite surf shop near the hotel where we were staying and met our instructor, Blackbear. One of the first tips he taught us was "On a paddleboard, if you look down, you fall down. Keep your focus on where you are going. Focus on the horizon; otherwise, the waves and big bounces will scare you, and you'll lose your concentration and end up in the water." I couldn't help but think how relevant that advice was to everyday living.

We spent the morning fulfilling the kids' dream of learning to paddleboard together as a family. We had a lot of laughs watching one another struggle to stay on the board at first, but then we all got the hang of it.

A couple of days later, I revisited our paddleboarding trip on the plane ride home with my son Steven. We spent much of the flight talking about Blackbear's wisdom and what we learned from our day of paddleboarding. When I asked Steven what that experience meant to him, he said, "If you're always looking at the big waves [the problem], you will always fall down." I thought about his insightful response and realized he was right. If you get stuck in the problems of today, you will be destined to fail because you will stay stuck exactly where you are—trapped in all of the small to-dos, time wasters, and pitfalls. But when you focus on the horizon—your vision—regardless of how rough the water can sometimes get, you will just keep paddling through life. When you know exactly where you're going, life's ride becomes easier to manage. It's your vision, your plan that takes you everywhere you want to go.

Step 4: Do the things that bring you power!

> "Do the thing and you will have the power. But they that not do not the thing, had not the power."
> —Ralph Waldo Emerson

Ralph Waldo Emerson had it right. I have found over the years that success is fundamentally predicated on finding what you are passionate about and then becoming relentless in your pursuit of every facet of that thing. To me, having the power means tapping into your greatest potential. It's what gives you the Michael Jordan drive, the fuel that feeds the engine to keep moving in the right direction in spite of the adversity and challenges you may meet along the way. Once you gain that power, you can focus on the new routines and rituals (i.e., do the things) that will create the success you desire.

This is where you get into what I call "inspired action," which is all the individual steps you must take to carry out your vision. This step is about creating structure in your life and doing things that bring you joy and power. This isn't just about a single area such as business or work. It includes all areas that make up your entire core.

When I first went to work for my father, I created a five-year plan that mapped out what I believed it would take to achieve my goal—running his company. It was a simple strategy. Year one was all about learning the back office of his operation. I worked with the receptionist, accountant, office administrator, the guys in the warehouse doing shipping and receiving, and learned every other job that started at the bottom until I knew I could effectively move on to sales. I wanted to know all about the business from the ground up. I figured that would give me an edge over the other people in the company who didn't have those same experiences to draw from.

By my third year in the company, I wanted to be a vice president of sales. Year four, I wanted to work in marketing, and year five, be president of the company. Interestingly enough, I didn't achieve that goal in five years, but I did finally achieve it after nine years. It took me the first five years to figure out that you have to be in action 365 days a year, doing the things that lead you to the eventual pot of gold in order to achieve that goal.

Looking back, I understand that my five-year plan was unrealistic. As I assessed my progress, I can say that I performed all of the right actions, but it took me four years longer of being in inspired action to become the person who earned that goal. The lesson I learned from this experience was to not be attached to the time frame but instead to fall in love with the process. This is one of the things that gives you the power and then leads you to your goal.

Whatever your vision, if you're miserable in the process—the *doing*—you will never find the power. You must embrace the action, the steps, and be present in the moment and with who you are on your way to becoming.

One of the ways I make myself okay with the process is by asking myself questions such as:

What do I love about doing this?

What do I love about who I am becoming?

What do I love about being disciplined?

Questions like this are designed to shift your focus away from the pain and toward the pleasure of meeting your goal.

When Deepak Chopra was a speaker at one of my seminars a few years back, he taught our group to be present each and every day by meditating for ten minutes and asking three questions:

1. Who are you?
2. What do you want?
3. What is your purpose in life?

I found it interesting that Deepak told the group *not* to answer the questions. Just ask them. For him, the process of asking is enough because the most important thing is to have a questioning attitude. It's what gives you insights that you would otherwise not have. I say, take that exercise one step further and answer the questions whenever you are in inspired action toward a goal or a vision.

If you get stuck, ask yourself some simple questions such as:

What gives my life power?

What can I do to change the previous outcome?

What can I change about my behavior to achieve my goals?

Success is predicated on finding what you are passionate about and then becoming relentless in your pursuit of every possibility so you will achieve your dreams. Track your results along the way and be open to making adjustments as you go. It's a process that may take multiple approaches before you find your sweet spot.

The better the questions, the better the answers.

Life is all about context and perspective. Every situation and circumstance is full of opportunity. The trick is figuring out how to see those openings and embrace the occasion. Carl Jung, the founder of analytic psychology, once said, "Perception is projection." How we feel on the inside radiates to the outside.

A big part of living By Design is radiating gratitude for what you have and an eagerness for more. This includes being grateful for your life being exactly where it is in this moment. Living each day grateful for the things we already have and not focusing on what we lack is a potent tool that gives us infinite power. Most people spend a lot of time reminding themselves of all the things that are missing instead of looking around and counting their blessings. They say things like "I hate my job," "I hate my relationship," "I hate how I look," and "I hate my life." Saying these things acknowledges everything that isn't working. Understand that everything we repeat attracts more of the same. It's the basic universal law that like attracts like.

I know that some of you who are reading this may be thinking, How can I be grateful that we are at war, that there is disease and famine, that I lost my life savings. I am not asking you to be grateful for those things. Rather, I am pointing out that you can be grateful for the men and women who are fighting for our freedom, grateful that you are not on the front lines, and grateful for having food even if you lost your savings.

Gratitude is an exercise in perspective. When I talk about gratitude to large crowds, I explain that how they listen to me over the course of those couple of hours will determine what they get out of my message and how it will impact their lives. If they are listening while thinking about their problems, everything they hear will amplify them. If, however, they are thinking about their goals and vision, everything I say will be in alignment with helping achieve those.

If you are willing to accept things for what they are, you must start by declaring that everything is perfect as it is but you are willing to improve. You are the one who got you where you are—likely by default. Now it is up to you to decide how you want your life to be, By Design.

My brother Matthew taught me a valuable lesson early in my sales career. When you make a mistake, no matter how big or small it is, declare it "perfect!" By doing so, you give yourself the power to learn from that mistake, find new solutions, develop better practices, and even create new systems to prevent it from happening again. It's a simple concept that often throws people a curve. Most people say, "You're crazy! How can I declare losing a big sale or an important relationship, or being fired from my job, perfect?" Of course, this argument comes only from people who have never tried it.

I was conducting one of my seminars a few years back when I shared the perfect game with the group I was talking to. The next morning, I asked people what they learned from the seminar the day before. One man stood and spoke with great enthusiasm. "I used that perfect thing yesterday and set three new business-building sales appointments—a three hundred percent improvement over my performance the day before." He explained that he had been waiting for his car in the valet line for thirty minutes when his phone rang. It was his daughter telling him that her car wouldn't start. Instead of becoming annoyed that he couldn't be there to help her, he thought Perfect! He quickly hung up the phone to call his insurance agent to confirm that he had towing insurance. After the agent said he did, he paused and said, "I'm glad you called. My wife and I are thinking about selling our home," and made an appointment before hanging up. Perfect!

The man then called his mechanic to have a tow truck sent to pick up his daughter. Before hanging up, he asked the mechanic if he had any real estate goals for the year.

Sure enough, the mechanic said he wanted to buy investment property.

Perfect! The man set up his second appointment in less than five minutes. By the time the tow truck pulled into the mechanic's shop, he was there to meet his daughter and the driver. After a few minutes of talking, the driver mentioned that he and his wife were saving up to buy their first home. He set up his third appointment—all thanks to his daughter's car breaking down!

Choose to declare everything that happens in life as perfect and see how the world opens up. Your shift in attitude alone will help you navigate life's ups and downs.

I play the perfect game every day because life happens. I have a buddy who recently told me about huge losses he has suffered in the stock market. He rattled off a number that made me weak in the knees, and yet he said it with calm and peace in his voice. He explained that he had no control over the stock market, no say in its ups or downs. He didn't get excited when the market was riding the wave of success, nor did he panic with the sudden loss. His balanced approach has helped him navigate his way through the treacherous waters. We can't control everything that happens in life, but we can control how we react to it. When a situation presents itself, it is our stimulus response that dictates the outcome.

So, what do you do to have the power?

1. Release: Who and/or what am I incomplete with? What do I need to let go of?
2. Gratitude: What am I grateful for now?
3. Declaration of my intentions: What do I want to attract and achieve?

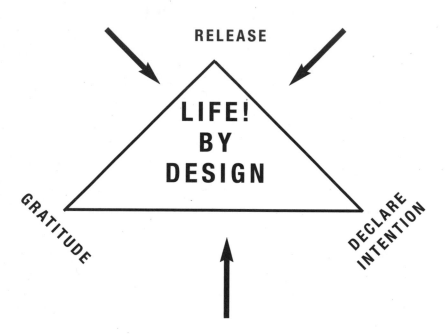

EQUALS LIFE BY DESIGN

I teach my clients to do something every morning that brings them power. If you do that, the rest of your day will automatically flow. For some people, that might be going to the gym. For others, it may call for daily affirmations, which are positive, present-tense statements that you make to yourself. It's all about creating the right mind-set for the day. Whatever your process, the idea is to begin each day with a clean slate.

I start out every morning by doing three things: I clean my slate by letting go of anything that happened in the past, and start my day without carrying over those emotions so I can begin each day with the clarity and focus I need to achieve my goals. I do this by writing out all the things I feel incomplete with or need to let go of. I follow the basic premise of not bringing yesterday into today's possibilities. I write down all the things I am grateful for or love about my life now. Once you are in a state of gratitude, you have shifted your focus to the extraordinary things in your life, which allows you to declare, with conviction and clarity, those things you want to attract in your life.

Next, I declare my intentions by practicing affirmations—simple, positive, present-tense statements I make that tell the truth about the future in advance. In Chapter 8, I explain in more detail the power of affirmations and how you can practice them.

The third action I take every morning is to note the things I most want to attract and achieve. I do this by implementing a detailed schedule or checklist each day that I approach with joy, passion, and enthusiasm. Even though I have been living By Design for years, I still map out my entire schedule, which includes my daily, weekly, monthly, and annual goals in great detail. I do this so I know exactly what I am committed to, where I'm headed, and how I plan to get there. My belief is, *If it's not on my schedule, it doesn't exist.*

I write entries on my calendar such as:

"6 p.m. Friday—Attend Michael's basketball game, practice shooting baskets with him before game, be present during game and be there for my son!"

"10 a.m. Tuesday—Coaching call with client—check on his relationship progress, new workout routine, personal achievements, number of sales calls made last week and how many of those translated into a sale. Inspire client to live By Design!"

Finding a perfect balance in your daily life can be challenging. Balance is different for everyone. Balance for a single guy living in New York City is different than it is for a married woman living in suburbia. If we don't define what being in balance means, we won't achieve it. If we don't acknowledge the things we want to accomplish, they'll never get done.

So, what is balance for you?

Answer the following question:

I'm in balance anytime I:

1.

2.

3.

4.

Single people may say they're in balance when they're exercising regularly, having fun with their friends, staying passionate in their work, and being in communication with their family and loved ones.

Married people with kids might say they're in balance anytime they're in communication with their spouse, in communication with their children, exercising regularly, spiritually connected to their faith, having fun or spending time with friends and family, and (if they work) feeling passionate about their career.

The key to achieving balance in life is knowing what it means to you and what it feels like to successfully live in balance. There is no right or wrong answer because balance is personal and subjective. Many people have unrealistic expectations about balance so they never feel as though they have it. Like all things we do By Design, we have to plan for balance to create it.

I also write down my intentions for each day so I have a clear picture of what I want to accomplish. It's as simple as this:

Intentions for today:

_____

_____

_____

_____

These three powerful elements—release, gratitude, and intention—are incorporated into my daily living, which not only give me the power but also help me maintain it. These three daily actions are designed to make me be completely present with how blessed my life already is, and help me stay connected, in sync, focused, and productive as a dad, husband, coach, and entrepreneur. My morning routine is about letting go of the past—acknowledging that it happened and then releasing from it. Doing this is powerful because it allows me to feel gratitude for all of my blessings.

Having a morning routine is a good start, but I see many people who are burned out by the end of their day. They've got nothing left to give to their relationships or their children, leaving those important people feeling unloved. Let's face it, we all fall into behavior patterns. We come home from a long day at work, maybe ask our loved one how his or her day was, talk to the kids for a few minutes about school, and then review our email, watch a football game or favorite show, and basically check out.

Are these activities bringing your other relationships power?

Engage with the people you love. Don't just ask, "How was your day, honey?" while looking at your BlackBerry. Stop. Put down the PDA. Look your spouse, your boyfriend, or girlfriend, and your kids in the eyes and be present. Become a part of their world. If you don't have kids, take your dog for a walk. Do at least one activity that requires you to be totally present and in the moment.

It's important to recognize that feeling good is the highest power.

You have to do things every day that create that sense. Several years ago I realized that although I was giving to all the people in my life, I wasn't doing anything for myself. From the outside looking in, life was good. But by October of every year, I would find myself so burned out that I had nothing left to give, with three months left to go before starting that cycle all over again.

It was time for the coach to get some coaching, so I hired a life coach I knew and respected. He started our first coaching session by asking me what activities I did that were purely "Tom time."

I couldn't come up with an answer. I had two young babies, and spent what little downtime I had with my wife while planning, creating, and working for our future. My coach wasn't surprised by my lack of response. He then asked me to tell him about any experience I'd had when I felt full of joy, where I wasn't doing anything other than being in the moment. My thoughts quickly turned to a recent trip I'd taken on a friend's sailboat. I told my coach about that spectacular day, how we sailed into the Pacific with a Frank Sinatra CD playing while I had the wheel and was just cruising along. There was something about being on the water, feeling the wind on my face, and being with a good friend that felt very Zen, peaceful, and full of joy.

My coach asked me why I wasn't creating moments like that every day.

"Because I don't own a sailboat," I said.

"You don't need a sailboat to create that experience. What you were attracted to by being on the boat were the couple of hours you had where no one was coming to you with questions, problems, worries, and concerns. You had 'quiet time' in that moment."

I had to think for several minutes about what my coach had just said. To test his theory, I spent my lunch hour for the next month walking down to the dock near my home and sitting by the sailboats in the harbor just being quiet. I gave myself sixty minutes of reflection time. I wasn't trying to solve any of life's great mysteries. Instead, I allowed my mind to be at peace and my body to just breathe. It was almost like being in a state of meditative nothingness. In the end, my coach was right on the money. Being next to the water, feeling the breeze and the sun on my skin, just as I had that day on the sailboat, was an effective and quiet way to recharge my batteries.

It is important to carve out "you" time every day. It doesn't have to be more than twenty minutes, as long as it is uninterrupted time you give yourself to recharge, rejuvenate, and reinvigorate. Surprisingly, it doesn't have to be alone time as long as you can be at peace. I have clients for whom tossing a baseball around with their son is all they need to find delight, passion, and joy. Be forewarned, checking email, Facebook, MySpace, Twitter, and messages is not what I am talking about here. What I mean is checking in with good friends, going for a run, meditating, reading, cooking, or doing whatever will give you extra power so you can go out and give more of yourself to the world.

EXERCISE

Knowing what you know about your goals, what activities or rituals would naturally and automatically fire you up to meet that goal? Make a list of the things that give *you* power personally and professionally. Declare all the things you're going to do on a daily basis to give yourself power—from making a tough sales call to becoming present in your relationship. What can you do to become more connected to your family, your body, your job, your intellectual self? What will you do to create your best life, By Design?

Most people I know are fanatical about making sure their cell-phone, iPod, or other personal devices are plugged in on a daily basis. They worry about being suddenly disconnected if the battery were to run down. If you're willing to give an electronic device this kind of daily care, why wouldn't you do it for yourself? Think of "you time" as plugging yourself into the wall and getting recharged.

Step 5: Practice visualizing yourself already there, in possession of what you want.

Just as highly trained athletes see themselves crossing the finish line, making that impossible putt, or winning first place, you must first visualize yourself as you choose to be. That's when you become the change you are seeking. If you can think it, act it. If you act it, you become it. That picture in your mind sets the tone for the outcome. Every detail matters—from the words you use to create the image to the desired outcome.

Faith is a gift that allows us to see things that aren't visible to the eye. Some people call this the gift of visualization, which is the process of creating a clear, sharp, emotionally charged mental movie of what you want to happen. It's imagining events as if they have already happened. It's a mental rehearsal of things to come.

When I first started my own business six years ago, my dear friend Nikki asked what my vision was for my new company. I described my ideas. Nikki listened closely as I spoke. When I finished, I thought I had given her a clear and precise picture of what I was trying to create.

"I noticed there are some elements missing from your vision, Tom. Would you like me to walk you through a visualization exercise to help you get a clearer, more detailed picture?" Nikki asked.

I was all for it. Nikki suggested I get comfortable and pointed to a chair across the room where I could relax and unwind. She told me to imagine a grounding cord coming from my spine and connecting me to the earth so I knew I would be safe. She suggested I create a beam of light to my right that I could grasp onto. It would be like an elevator that would take me both up and down.

She then directed me to see myself floating up beyond the building we were sitting in and into the clouds, where I could see the skyline of the city. She told me to keep floating upward, past the atmosphere, up to the stars, where I could look down at the little ball below that was Earth.

Once I felt comfortable, Nikki suggested I ride the beam of light back down to Earth. But when I returned this time, it would be twenty years into the future. She wanted me to notice the city I was seeing. Was it a different city than when I left? What did I notice about the skyline? How had it changed? And where was I about to land? Was it someplace new? Was it my home or an office or some other environment I had never been to before?

Once I hit the ground, I described what I saw. I'd landed in a university setting, more like what I imagine the Apple campus to look like rather than a major university such as UCLA. I could see lots of professional people running around among several buildings—an equal number of men and women as well as kids. It felt like its own little self-enclosed city. I realized that this was one of *my* universities that helped people live By Design.

When Nikki asked me to leave that setting and go to where I lived, I described a Spanish-style home on the beach. When I saw the house from the street, I couldn't see if it was beachfront, but I could tell that the house was near the ocean because seagulls were flying overhead. My wife, Kathy, greeted me at the front door. She looked as beautiful as she did the day I married her. Nikki encouraged me to get present by engaging all five of my senses with what I was seeing. What did Kathy look like? What was Kathy wearing? How did the house smell?

When I walked through the front door, I noticed that I was in the courtyard. Twenty years into the future, I had some gray hair but looked pretty much the same. I was wearing a casual shirt, untucked, with shorts and sandals. When I looked out the window, I saw my son Michael holding a baby. When I realized it was *his* baby, my eyes welled up. Michael's wife was there, along with my other son, Steven, having a great time as grown men. The collective joy I felt was overwhelming.

Finally, Nikki steered me toward having a conversation with my future self. I was excited by the opportunity to ask questions of myself twenty years from now. I began rattling off whatever came into my head:

What has the journey been like for the past twenty years?

What advice would you give me today to help me allow myself to organically get here versus forcing it?

What were some of the most important lessons you learned along the way?

What advice would you give me when I run into hardship?

What do the grandchildren call me?

At the end of the questions, I gave my future self a long hug and said goodbye to all my loved ones. I walked outside, found my beam of light, and brought myself back to the present.

The first time I did this visualization was one of the most powerful experiences I have ever had. I wrote down every detail of what I saw and felt. The essence of my original vision for my new company never changed, but I got more pieces of the puzzle, which allowed me to tweak my vision toward what I saw.

When you practice visualizing, the more detail you can see, the clearer you will be to create your vision. The overriding message I got from that vision is that my life will be fantastic. Even when things get hard, I understood that I didn't need to spend one minute worrying about it because when something happens that may jolt me from my beliefs, I know it's supposed to happen. Life isn't automatic or without challenges and bumps along the way. If it was that simple, we'd all be living our vision already. Regardless of the circumstances, that exercise taught me to enjoy each moment of every day because the result will be worth it. I have since led tens of thousands of people at my seminars through this particular visualization because I felt so strongly about the impact it had on my life and vision.

Many people I work with think they can't visualize. They don't know how to do it or can't slow down their thoughts and pause to get a clear picture in their heads. Whenever I hear those statements, my first response is to tell them to close their eyes and visualize an apple.

"Did an elephant appear when you did that? Or did a red or green apple show up?" I ask. If an apple is what they saw, then they can visualize. Visualization is a learned skill. It takes practice and patience, but it is a powerful tool to help you reach your goals.

As in the story of Ben Comen, many noted achievers have mastered the art of visualization. I play a lot of golf and I have a tendency to sink more putts when I can visualize the ball dropping into the cup. Jack Nicklaus once said he never hit a shot in golf without first having a sharp picture of it in his head. We become what we practice in our minds. If we imagine failure, it will come. If we imagine success, it will come. One of the key elements in creating your vision is to see in your mind the exact way you want things to go.

VISUALIZATION EXERCISE #1

I want you to imagine a lemon. What does it look like? What does it smell like? What does it taste like? Some of you might pucker at the mere thought of a lemon. How did you respond?

A study done a few years ago tested the idea of visualization. The study divided a basketball team into two groups. The first group was asked to go onto the court and practice tossing free throws; the second group sat in their locker room and visualized making their shots. Which group do you think did better when they tested their accuracy?

The group that had visualized the free throws shot a higher percentage than the other group. Why? Because when you visualize, you have 100 percent accuracy. You see the process unfold as you connect the shot every time, and that translates into increasing your success rate when actually performing the task at hand.

STOP! If you knew you could increase your ability to perform and achieve what you want to achieve by simply closing your eyes and seeing it happen, why aren't you doing it every day? Does this need to be added to your list of "Things that give me power"?

I can hear you saying to yourself, "I know, I know. I've heard this before."

Here's my answer. Your addiction to the past is what stops you from visualizing on a daily basis. Why? I am guessing you tried it once and it didn't work. Or you tried it once but never slowed down enough to be present and clear so you didn't get the results you wanted. Perhaps someone told you that visualization was for "out there" self-helpers, and because you care about the opinion of others, that stopped you cold. Am I on the right track?

Hello! We are talking about living your life By Design—not by default. The number of people who visualize on a daily basis might match the number of people who are currently living By Design. Are you ready to be a Peyton Manning, an Oprah Winfrey, or even the boss or teacher you look up to?

Visualization requires you to free your mind and clear any thoughts that might make it difficult for the subconscious mind to receive mental pictures. For some of you, this might require finding a quiet space where you can really open up without any interruptions. This obviously means turning off your television, cellphone, or PDA; having your assistant hold your calls; and closing your bedroom or office door or waiting for the kids to go down for a nap.

Since your subconscious mind is most receptive to new information first thing in the morning and in the evening before you go to sleep, I suggest practicing your visualization skills at either (or both) of these times every day. Close your eyes and focus on your breathing. Take deep, rhythmic breaths through your nose and then exhale through your mouth. Try to feel each breath as it enters and then leaves your body. I tell my clients to think of a lake they've been to and then imagine the rippling water as they toss in a pebble. Once you're in a relaxed and peaceful state, you can begin to visualize in the present tense, as if whatever you're seeing is already happening. See your image, hear it, taste it, smell it, and really feel it. The clearer the picture, the clearer your vision will be.

VISUALIZATION EXERCISE #2

Imagine yourself in the perfect relationship, in perfect shape, or in the perfect job. What does it look like? How does it make you feel?

The process of visualization is the beginning of creating positive change. If you can't yet answer the questions in Visualization Exercise #2, don't panic. You are not without hope. You can and will be able to answer them in no time. You need to get connected with the picture you are creating in your mind. This is called *creating your vision*. The important thing to remember as you talk yourself through the visualization process is to create good feelings while you're doing it. This emotionally anchors you to your vision. The hardest part for most people is holding the thought as they want it to be. Many times, people allow their thoughts to drift away from the vision, causing them to see more of what they don't want.

6 STEPS TO EFFECTIVE VISUALIZATIONS

1. Get over your fear, addictions, and drama.
2. Get relaxed.
3. See things as you want them to be.
4. Engage as many senses as possible.
5. Feel good while holding the result in your mind.
6. Stay energized by seeing your vision throughout the day.

For more powerful guided visualizations, check out Kelly Howell, www.brainsync.com. I really admire her work and use her visualization technique myself.

Make sure you keep your visualizations positive and energized throughout the day by staying enthusiastic and believing in the possibilities. Resist connecting any negative feeling to your visualizations by reinforcing them with positive self-talk, believing every word you speak. You will gain the most benefit from your visualizations when you confidently and clearly expect them to happen. The more you practice, the easier it will be to continuously put yourself in a state of already being there. You're creating a strong emotional anchor and a pull toward the accomplishment of your vision. See it everywhere you go. If you're consistent and persistent, you will be amazed at how effective visualization is. You will notice that you are making things possible in your life that you once doubted. With practice and patience, you will find that your success rate will dramatically increase by utilizing visualization techniques. Remember that the process takes time, so don't get frustrated if you don't see results right away.

Step 6: Create structure and accountability by telling others around you about your plans.

Creating structure and accountability is a powerful tool that can keep you on the right track. There are two kinds of people in the world: people who will support your new choices, and people who will love to see you fail (the defaulters). Both can be terrific motivators. Remember, success is the best revenge! The more people you tell about your plan, the more accountable you become to succeed. Since most people are addicted to the opinions of others, they don't want to be perceived as a failure by family, friends, or peers. That is why creating accountability is one of the best ways to stay on your path and help you get over your addiction.

I have been living By Design for twenty years, which has taken me to an expert level of awareness and the need to start each day in the right frame of mind. Although I don't expect you to jump in at this level, I want to share my daily routine, which sets the tone for everything else that follows. My first phone call of the day is usually to an affirmation partner, who is like a workout buddy. You are there to encourage and motivate each other without judgment. Lisa came to me as a client in January 2009. She'd had a moderately successful year but was worried that things might take a turn for the worse. I could tell she already felt as if she had fallen off track. What Lisa needed was someone she could talk to on a daily basis to help get her out of her head and away from her doubts and insecurities. I suggested she become my affirmation partner because she had a good plan in place but still needed some mental reinforcement to stay on her path and follow her vision. Lisa would affirm her financial goals, relationship goals, connection with family, fitness goals, and the things that gave her the power to meet these goals. We spoke only for five to ten minutes every morning, but it helped us both start off our day in a positive frame of mind.

My next phone call is with my "Ten Daily Questions" buddy. Every morning we ask each other ten questions that are designed to keep us both authentic and on track. We customize our questions, which means that mine vary slightly from his. As we progress, some of our Core Seven areas need more accountability than others, so we make the appropriate tweaks as we go. We engage in this routine only on workdays, usually Monday through Friday. Our answers are limited to "yes" or "no." No explanations or stories allowed. The value of this daily exercise is to quickly gauge where you're at and make you accountable to someone else with your answers.

My buddy's questions are the following:

1. Did you live By Design yesterday?
2. Did you have a sweat-breaking workout?
3. Did you take 100 percent responsibility for the passion in your relationship?
4. Did you slow down and connect with each son and be present to his needs?
5. Did you give yourself any Tom time?

6. Did you start off your day with gratitude and clarity?

7. Did you manage your wealth and create more of it?

8. Are you incomplete with anything? Is there anyone you need to reach out to?

9. Did you make any new contacts yesterday to build your business?

10. Did you lead, delegate, and inspire the team around you?

By question ten, I have a clear idea of whether or not I am in inspired action and pursuing my vision. If I rattle off a bunch of "no's" in a row, chances are I'm off my path and I'd better do something to get back in line. This exercise is a quick way for me to gauge where I am, what areas of my life need tending, and what areas I'm avoiding.

Occasionally, we add a couple of extra questions at the end of our lists of ten. The first is "Did you end the day with silent meditation and appreciation for life and everyone around you?" This question is dropped in to remind each other to live with gratitude every day, something everyone needs to become aware of and practice. (Later I delve into why this is so important.)

The second add-on is "Did you lie to me?"

This is always a bit of a "I'm calling you out" question because we aren't allowed to give explanations in our answers. So if either of us lies to the other, clearly we are not living the vision and are so uncomfortable by that failure that we are covering it up. The whole idea is to create accountability for our daily actions, even if we need to be called on the carpet.

When creating accountability, the ultimate liability is money. It's a source of angst and one of the hardest things for people to part with, especially when it's a penalty. Money makes people think they no longer have the option of giving up, motivating them to create structure and accountability in their plan.

To create this kind of accountability, I've asked clients to write out

If you really need change and you're stuck in a rut, money talks. Put yourself on a strict accountability program.

checks for each goal they want to achieve. Sometimes the amount is small, say a hundred dollars, and other times I've asked for much larger sums, up to fifty thousand dollars. The amount needs to be painful for those writing the check, whether they're a multimillionaire or someone aspiring to be. For every goal they reach, I return a check. For every failed attempt, I send the check to someone they'd never want the money to go to, such as a rival in business, a competitor, an ex-lover, or an organization they would otherwise never make a donation to. I made one client write out his checks to his exwife. Our deal was this: If he didn't achieve his desired goal, each check would be sent with a letter that read, "Dear Honey, I found some extra cash. If you need more, just call." He worked twenty-four hours a day, seven days a week, to make sure all of his goals were achieved. He couldn't stand the idea of his ex-wife getting an extra penny more than she'd already gotten in their divorce. The thought of me giving a check to his ex-wife was the motivation he needed, and the structure and accountability he required, to not quit until he reached his goal.

If you want to test this approach for yourself, the next time you say you want to lose weight, start a workout plan or establish any other goal, write a check to someone you don't respect along with a note that reads, "Dear friend, I just wanted you to know I've looked up to and admired you for years. I have silently observed you and have learned so many lessons by the way you move through the world. I know I could never repay my debt of gratitude, but I thought this money would be a good start."

Put the letter and check in a preaddressed envelope and give it to someone you trust to hold it for you. Next, tell them your goal—to lose twenty pounds by July 17 or go to the gym four days a week, whatever. If you haven't reached that goal, tell them to put the letter in the mail, no questions asked. The next time you reach for that cookie, ice cream, or stack of pancakes and order of bacon, or hit the snooze button on your alarm clock to stay in bed rather than get up and work out, ask yourself the following questions: "Is that food or sleep worth sending my money? Does that one burst of pleasure and joy mean more to me than the money I've sealed in that envelope?" I guarantee that suddenly food won't taste as good, or those few extra minutes of sleep won't mean as much. That will be the beginning of real change.

Over the years, I have sent out numerous checks that clients have written, for as much as a thousand dollars. And although I've never sent out one for fifty grand, I came close with a client a few years back. He was extremely talented and owned several multimillion-dollar companies. He needed to make a quantum leap in business by finding a replacement for himself in each of his corporations. He loved being a micromanager but recognized that his management style was actually a trap because it prevented his companies from growing. His negative pattern was to hire managers and various other leaders, empower them, and then fire them within a year because they weren't meeting his expectations. Of course, they were failing because he was micromanaging these experts and not allowing them to do their jobs.

We agreed that he would profile the right people for the jobs and hire them without the possibility of firing them for two years. Our deal was this: If he fired any of his new managers because of his micromanaging ways, his check for fifty thousand dollars would be sent to an organization he despised. This was an extreme measure, but it worked. We changed a major fault in his leadership style and, in the process, increased the productivity and profitability of his companies.

Crazy?

You bet. But what's even crazier is to keep repeating the same cycles and continuing to live by default. Think about your life twenty years from now. Are you crazy because you agreed to my radical plan or crazy because you didn't and remained stuck in your old ways?

If you've ever gone on a diet and quit, if you've ever made a New Year's resolution and not seen it through, if you've ever set forth a goal or an intention and gave up partway through, what was missing from the equation that allowed you to give up? I guarantee it was structure and accountability.

They are what hold your vision together on the days you don't feel up to it. They are what get you to the office on the days you'd rather call in sick. They are what make me do my affirmations on the days I don't feel like doing them, and make me get up and speak to a crowd of forty people when I was expecting fifteen hundred and still be ready and present for them. Structure and accountability are designed to save you from the consequences of not doing something.

It has taken years to refine the process of living By Design and move it from twenty steps to six steps. My clients look for fast results. If you want to make a shift from living by default to living By Design in any area of your life, follow these six steps. I promise you, my friend, there is so much joy and possibility for you on the other side. I know you've read books like this before. I know you've been down this path before. Give yourself the gift of one more disciplined experiment. And this time, see it through—free of the four addictions that have held you back in the past—and experience the true joy and endless possibilities you were meant to have in your life.

EXERCISE

Write down your three most important goals. Now, apply the 6 Steps to Living By Design to be present with what you want. Read these steps with the idea of bringing you closer to your goals rather than amplifying all the things that are holding you back.

THE CONSCIOUS AND SUBCONSCIOUS MIND AND THE POWER OF SELF-TALK

What if I could teach you to control almost every aspect of your future? Do you want that kind of power? Of course you do. That is why you are reading this book. But if all you're doing is reading and not acting, you will never break the cycle of living by default. To begin living By Design, you have to be willing to turn your thinking around and take control of your thoughts, or they will continue to control you.

There's nothing new about the subject of positive thinking, yet many people still fill their brain with mostly negative thoughts. Your thoughts are created by your belief system. Your success in all areas of life—personal, work, spiritual, relationships—is determined, for the most part, by the power of your beliefs, what you tell yourself about yourself. Self-talk, which consists of your innermost thoughts and actual words you say to yourself, goes on all the time. Learning to control your internal communication will limit the negativity in your life.

Your subconscious mind is like a hard drive in a computer. It stores every old action and old behavior—everything positive and negative that has happened in your life. The primary overriding thought your subconscious mind has is to protect you and keep you safe. So when you become aware of a problem in your relationship, for example, your subconscious mind immediately pulls up old data to support or advise against, say, making a decision to have a difficult conversation with your partner. It isn't natural for anyone to purposely put themselves in a place of fear, pain, and anguish. Yet sometimes the actions we have to take require us to break through that subconscious protective barrier.

Your conscious mind is made up of words, thoughts, actions, and everyday behaviors. So if I tell you to take action and go clean up that relationship, your subconscious mind fires off lots of excuses for not going through with it. For example, you might say something like, "The one time I brought up this issue, my spouse got really upset with me. We got into a really bad argument. I felt terrible afterward and vowed never to bring it up again. Forget it. I'll just keep doing what I'm doing."

> The mind cannot differentiate between real or imagined thoughts. This makes *all* thoughts real, whether true or not.

Numerous studies have proven that the conscious mind can hold only one thought at a time, either positive or negative. If you're not thinking a positive thought, you are, by default, thinking a negative one. Most of us have been programmed to think a certain way and are greatly influenced by everything around us, from the environment in which we live and work to the people we encounter on a daily basis.

Most people are comfortable with the thoughts they regularly have and then spend their time reinforcing those thoughts because they believe them to be true. Self-talk—either spoken or unspoken—can take the form of feelings, emotions, or actual physical responses. Think about how you feel when you're excited or nervous about something. Your heart races with anticipation. This is a physical reaction to a thought you're having.

Our minds are constantly in thought, even when we are sleeping. Most of our self-talk is unconscious, meaning we aren't even aware of it. Every thought we have is tied to something we already know from our past. It could be something we've seen, heard, smelled, tasted, judged, analyzed, or experienced. Once our brain takes in new information, it starts an almost instant process of categorizing that information and tying it to something we already know so we can react to it. That is why we instinctively know when to accept, believe, doubt, approve, disapprove, or otherwise respond to something.

Your subconscious mind remembers everything. It accepts whatever statements we make and acts accordingly. If everything you say to yourself is believed, then every time you send a negative thought to your subconscious mind, it accepts it as true and acts on it. You would never sit down at your computer and type the word, "Crash," "Lose my files," or "Lose all of my contacts," right? So why would you send the same kind of messages to your brain? Think of your conscious thoughts as the keyboard to your computer. Every thought you have becomes a message to your brain. If you keep feeding yourself the wrong information, you will never be able to make things right. Unless you change your internal program by turning your negative self-talk into positive self-talk, you will not be able to change your results.

When I was twenty-one years old, my mentor Bill Mitchell gave me good advice based on his growing up on a farm in Michigan. He said the greatest lesson he learned was if you plant corn, you don't get tomatoes.

At first, I had no idea what he was talking about.

He explained that if you plant only doubt, lack, limitation, and fear in your mind, you won't ever end up with love, success, wealth, abundance, and prosperity. How you think and react to a stimulus clearly dictates the outcome.

Okay. Hold on. Do you find yourself thinking more positive or negative thoughts? Be honest.

Your self-concept is how you view yourself. What you see when you look in the mirror and what thoughts go through your head are all images of your self-concept. We have self-concepts about everything in life, including our appearance, relationships, eating habits, work ethic, parenting skills, how much money we make, and how others view us.

The words we say to ourselves are extremely powerful. They can make us laugh, cry, think, and act. They can create or destroy. When you verbalize a thought, an emotional attachment is formed. That bond can motivate you to leap into inspired action or keep you from ever getting off the couch. This is why it is crucial to think about what you are going to say before you speak. Once words are uttered, they're hard to take back, especially words we say to ourselves.

Are your thoughts and choice of words building you up or tearing you down? Everything you tell yourself becomes a directive to your subconscious mind. Most people who use negative self-talk aren't even aware they're doing it. Here are some examples:

1. I'm fat.
2. I can't . . .
3. Why does this keep happening to me?
4. I'm so stupid/I'm an idiot.

5. I don't have the time.

6. I wish . . .

7. If only . . .

The list is never-ending.

Negative self-talk is one of the most debilitating self-inflicted acts we can do to ourselves. The good news is that it's a habit that can be unlearned. The bad news is that most people find it easier to be self-loathing, saying things like "poor me" and "feel sorry for me," and therefore stay that way. One thing is for certain: We are our worst critics. If you're like many of the people I speak to every day, you've had countless sleepless nights wondering where your life is going. Most of the time your thoughts are negative, which seems to make matters even worse than they appeared during the day. And before you know it, you've created all sorts of scenarios that simply don't exist.

Most people have a hard time giving up negative self-talk. The habit is hard to break because it requires a strong desire to make the necessary changes and then take action. The secret is more about awareness than effort. Negative thoughts are often based on preconceived ideas. Changing how you view them is the first step to seeing these same circumstances as positive experiences. Once you learn to reject self-limiting beliefs, they lose their power over you. When you change your self-talk, you change your self-concept, which unleashes all of your unlimited potential.

The only real limitations you have in life are the ones you place on yourself. You limit your potential when you focus your energy on re-inforcing negative messages. According to research psychologists, the average one-year-old child has a three-word vocabulary. By fifteen months, children can speak about nineteen words. At two years of age, most kids possess a working knowledge of 272 words. Age three, 896 words; age four, a little over 1,500 words. Our word accumulation continues to grow. The average adult speaks around 18,000 words a day. Sigmund Freud said, "Words have a magical power. They can bring either the greatest happiness or deepest despair; they can transfer knowledge from teacher to student . . ." This is why it is so important to choose your words By Design!

EXERCISE

Make a list of all the common negative self-talk statements you make during the day. Next, reword them to become positive statements. For example, if you say, "I don't understand technology," change it to say, "I love technology and am excited to learn new things every day." If you say, "My spouse doesn't give me the attention I want," let it become "I love my spouse and I take one hundred percent responsibility for the love in my relationship." Do you hear the difference in these statements? One is living as a victim, by default; the other is living as a victor, By Design.

In order to change your negative thought patterns, you must learn to limit negativity in your life. One effective method I use to start the process is replacing those old self-beliefs with positive, present-tense, By Design thoughts throughout the day. Some people refer to such statements as affirmations. Brian Tracy first exposed me to affirmations in 1989. His message was that if I wanted to increase my self-esteem and self-image and strengthen my vision, I must affirm the things I want.

Before you roll your eyes at me, understand that your doubt is, in and of itself, an affirmation. Think about it. Affirmations can be both positive and negative. If you say "my back hurts," "I can't," or "I'm so fat," you're creating a negative affirmation every day. The real question is, are you doing it by default or By Design?

Because you decide how your mind works, you may as well feed it positive thoughts, right? Even though we have all heard the statement "You are what you think," few people understand the value of doing positive affirmations, let alone allocating the time to do them.

When affirmations are used to reinforce positive feelings, they induce a calm, confident attitude that provides a sense that everything will be all right. Affirmations can open your channels of creativity and allow you to let go of the pressures you feel throughout the day. In the process, you release the negative energy, tension, anxiety, and other pessimistic emotions that hold you back.

Some people view prayer as the highest form of affirmation, while others simply prefer to call it positive self-talk. Whatever you want to call it, the methods used to practice positive affirmations are effective and reliable. The process is akin to working out. You have to exercise your positive self-belief to keep your mind and spirit in top condition. If I go a few days without practicing affirmations, I feel as though I've missed a few days at the gym. I don't feel as sharp, strong, or focused.

In the early days of my affirmations, I'd make my statements simple but to the point, saying things like:

I believe in myself.

I like myself.

I believe in what I think.

I am a goal achiever.

As lame as those statements sound to me today, at the time I didn't like myself. I didn't believe in me. I was still wearing five earrings and had just gotten rid of my Mohawk. I was coming from years of doubt, lack, and limitation. You can plant a seed, but if the ground isn't fertile, the seed may not grow. I needed to reprogram my self-image and self-esteem—big-time!

At Brian Tracy's suggestion, I began doing affirmations on my way to work. I rode my 125 cc motorcycle and screamed at the top of my lungs for the entire ride, "I Like Myself!" "I Believe in Me!" and so on, over and over. By the time I got to work, I found that my day went by faster, I accomplished more, and I was building my self-image and my self-esteem.

Affirmations became even more important to me a couple of years after I went to work for my father, when I began working as a salesman for his company. I love the saying "When you know something but don't apply it, it is as if you have never learned it at all." I recognized the power of affirming thoughts because I got immediate benefits from doing my affirmations. For the first time in my life, I felt good. I wanted to do whatever I could to keep that feeling, so I upped my statements to reinforce my new role, saying "I am a powerful salesperson," "I attract great clients," and "People love to do business with me." And even though I was met with rejection along the way, I continued to affirm the results I was seeking until I got them.

You can create affirmations for every area of your life. They can be about yourself, your family, your career, your finances, and even your spirituality. Affirmations are easy to do and can be practiced anywhere, anytime, and as often as you need them. You want to make sure you can visualize the desired outcome and feel the emotion, as if you are already what you see in your mind's eye. Research has shown that your subconscious mind reacts most positively to from ten to fifteen affirmations at a time, but don't worry about overloading your brain if you have more statements than that. The goal is to retrain your thoughts to help you see life in a better, more positive light.

Affirmations can either be written down, repeated silently to yourself, or said out loud. A written affirmation is a list of positive, precise, present-tense statements that should be definitive and reflect your exact vision or desired outcome. They are short and powerful statements such as:

1. I attract new accounts every day.
2. I weigh 145 pounds and love my body.
3. I am a powerful and decisive leader.
4. I am the best (father, mother, swimmer, cook, partner, marketer).

Hold on for a minute. I know some of you might be thinking I sound like Stuart Smalley from *Saturday Night Live*. I hear you because I have those same thoughts. But after twenty years of practicing affirmations, and witnessing thousands of clients go from a negative spiral to being back on track, I must tell you something. If you want to live By Design, affirmations are a must. Why? Because they work!

Choosing your words By Design will help you release from the past and the drama that surrounds your life. Why? Because you will declare everything you want in the present tense as if it is already happening.

Another effective method is to read your list to yourself or out loud. Hearing your statements cements their validity and importance in your life. As you make these confirming statements, try to visualize each one as if it were already happening. When you believe your thoughts, you will walk, talk, and act as though they are already a part of your being.

As I reflect on my life, I can honestly say that I've achieved everything I've affirmed for 90 to 120 days. I am a huge believer in setting forth your intentions by speaking about them in a positive way.

Although affirmations had become a part of my daily routine, they took on a whole new meaning the first time my wife announced we were pregnant. I thought, This is the ultimate opportunity to take my affirmations further, to give them all the power and impact they can have on my life. I wanted to create affirmation tapes for my unborn child to hear in the womb so he would develop with only positive reinforcement and unconditional love. So I wrote down all the positive statements I could think of in the present tense about my unborn son, his health, and what I wished for him after he was born. I set those affirmations to Baroque classical music and played it daily for the baby in my wife's belly. I made statements including:

1. I love you.
2. You are *my* son.
3. You have a happy heart.
4. You have healthy lungs.
5. You have healthy organs.
6. You have a healthy liver.

I affirmed everything I could think of—except his eyes. Michael was a healthy baby, but he was diagnosed with strabismus, a vision problem in which the two eyes do not look at the same point at the same time. You may think I'm out of my mind for feeling guilty about my son's condition, but I honestly feel that if I had affirmed that he be born with healthy eyes and would see with perfectly clear vision, he would not have had this condition. Thankfully, it was repairable. Two surgeries later, Michael can now see perfectly.

When my wife shared the good news that we were expecting again a couple of years later, I was a lot more intentional and specific in affirming this baby's health. Steven was born perfectly healthy, with no medical issues.

The daily practice of making affirmations begins the process of unlocking the power of your subconscious mind.

I have a good friend with whom I share a lot of similar interests. We own a boat together and enjoy hanging out with our children. One day he overheard my oldest son talking to his son about a mutual friend the kids knew from school. My buddy's son said he "hated that kid." I have always taught my kids that "hate" is a powerful word that shouldn't be used lightly. My son told the other little boy that he didn't hate their friend—he loved him. Then he said, "I love myself, I love my daddy, I love school, I love learning, and I love you!" My son isn't a geek or a nerd. He is a young man whose parents have instilled positive affirmations into his vernacular, which makes him different, but in a good way.

Later that evening, my friend approached me and said, "Dude, you're brainwashing your kid." My response was "You're right. Better me than society—better me than SpongeBob!" My friend is a neurosurgeon; he does up to fifteen brain surgeries a week. He's brilliant! And yet he hasn't learned an important secret about the organ he operates on. If we continually plant doubt, lack, limitation, and fear in our minds, we don't grow, succeed, and have healthy lives full of abundance and love.

Some of you might be thinking I'm filling my children's minds with ideas and dreams they may never achieve, yet all dreams start with your thoughts and beliefs, which create the desire and courage to act. The sooner we can load a child's brain with positive beliefs, the more successful that child will become. A child who believes that anything is possible has been given the greatest gift imaginable—the ability to dream big.

EXERCISE

Get a package of 150 cards and for the next thirty days write five positive, affirming statements about yourself—one statement on each card. Make sure your statements are in the present tense and are clear in intention. Say them out loud with confidence and conviction. Review them twice a day until each statement has become a reality.

When I want to take my affirmations to the next level, I practice them with a little Tom Ferry twist. I call them affirm-actions.™ Here's the difference. Affirmations comprise positive self-talk, phrases such as "I like myself," "I'm alive, excited, and full of energy," and "I earn a million dollars a year!"

Affirm-actions™ connect the body and mind because your whole body is physically involved in the process. Your body and mind can then work together to create and firmly implant the new positive thought. A body in motion remains in motion. Lots of actors, politicians, public speakers, and top businesspeople regularly use this mental and physical combination. It could include clapping, touching, pumping your fists, or whatever works to get your whole body and mind present, in the moment, and centered.

Affirm-actions™ are a self-induced pep talk to get you ready for whatever you are about to encounter. For example, when I am preparing a lecture or presentation, I stand up offstage, just before I address my audience, and I clap my hands and say "I'm alive, present, and full of energy!" By doing this, I create a new level of energy all around me that is carried throughout my presentation and beyond.

I tell myself that I am grateful, focused, fearless, powerful, unstoppable, and willing to do whatever it takes *right now*! This quick method is also effective in preparing for any meeting, challenge, or event of importance. It will put you in the right frame of mind to be most effective and engaging. When you get your body involved, the mind will follow.

Affirm-actions can be practiced by a series of mental exercises that stimulate your subconscious mind and accelerate the results of making inner changes in your life. When you add a physical response to these self-affirming statements, you engage your entire body in the process. Repeating these thoughts daily is the fastest way to reprogram your negative thoughts into positive ones.

Today, both of my sons are extremely confident and comfortable in front of adults and large groups because I have been conditioning them since before day one. We do affirm-actions together all the time. I'll occasionally walk into their room and unexpectedly ask them for their daily affirmations. They'll shout out whatever they're thinking.

"I'm happy!"

"I'm powerful!"

"I'm focused!"

"I love school!"

"I love learning!"

"I'm a great speaker!"

I love hearing their positive thoughts and knowing they keep a healthy frame of mind. One night while I was traveling for a seminar, my cellphone rang. It was my wife calling to say that our son Michael wanted to tell me a story. He presented about a five-minute speech he had given at school earlier that day. He had been feeling a tremendous amount of pressure because if he did well, his speech would be recorded and played for the entire student body at the end of the school year. Michael explained that his goal going into his speech was to make it onto that video. He had a vision. He knew what he wanted and was aware of what he needed to do to achieve it. I could not have been prouder.

Michael continued with his story. "Right before I was supposed to give my speech, I noticed I wasn't feeling well. For whatever reason, my hands were sweaty and I didn't feel right. I walked outside the classroom for a couple of minutes and told myself, 'I'm a great presenter. I'm powerful. I'm focused. And I'm going to make the video reel!' I clapped my hands together to get really psyched. I repeated the statements over and over until I felt good. I walked back into the room, and I nailed it, Dad!"

I told Michael how proud I was. I said he'd given me a great story to share at my seminar the next day. To my surprise, Michael paused and got quiet. He usually shares my enthusiasm when he tells me about his accomplishments. But this time, something was bothering him.

"What is it, buddy?" I asked.

"Daddy, I have to tell you something that might upset you. I don't like it when you *make* me do affirmations." With those words, I went from being the proudest father in the world to feeling that I had somehow forced my son into something he didn't want to do. Even though I knew I was instilling the right values by teaching him ways to create positive self-esteem and self-worth, hearing his doubt hurt my heart. I asked him to explain why he felt that way.

He said, "I don't like it when I'm in the backseat of the car while you're driving to my basketball practice and you make me say, 'I'm a great rebounder and I play great defense.'" It felt like Michael was suddenly mocking me.

"I don't like it when you force me to do them, Dad. But I have to tell you something else. I'm really happy that you do because when I need them, they're there."

My heart was again full of love and joy. Later that night, I called my wife to tell her that we were doing a really good job with our kids. I was thrilled to know that my ten-year-old son was more prepared for life than the average adult is by age forty. This was an extremely proud moment for me as a father and the ultimate example of "Do the thing and you will have the power." It was extremely satisfying to know that my kids reinforce their positive thoughts on a daily basis.

HEALTHY BODY, HEALTHY MIND

By now, you might be asking yourself, "Does this guy ever sleep?" I'm sure many of you are convinced that I must still be on drugs to operate at this level and live this lifestyle. But I'm not. If you're feeling the pressure of how do I fit all of this in and do all the things you're asking me to do, one of the reasons is because you probably lack the energy required to get it all done. I know I am not the first, nor will I be the last to say to you, "Healthy body, healthy mind." But be clear: If you want to sustain a life By Design, your health, vitality, and mental and emotional toughness are a must.

Most people get stuck in their lives because they lack the energy and vitality to push through. They get complacent, lazy, and lethargic, and have no stamina to endure the day. These conditions are all effects of a much bigger cause. They didn't properly fuel their body by eating right, doing the emotional work to give themselves the boost they need throughout the day, and getting enough rest to recharge and reinvigorate.

Having enough energy is a choice. You can either submit to a lack of stamina and excessive fatigue or you can do something to improve your overall vitality. A buddy of mine is extremely successful, one of the top executives in his field, and was, by most people's standards, living an extraordinary life. The only thing holding him back was his weight—over 350 pounds. His health had become so compromised and he had become so uncomfortable that he could no longer sleep with his wife. After years of emotional and physical neglect, his wife filed for divorce. By professional standards, my friend was hugely successful. But was his life successful?

This is why choosing to take care of your body is as important as nurturing your mind. Everything we do starts with our health and vitality. My philosophy on health is based on doing whatever we can to not only bolster but maintain a high level of energy throughout the day. I am talking about a supreme level of energy from the moment you swing your feet onto the floor first thing in the morning until you fall back into bed at night.

When you don't feel good, your attitude is off and your actions are subpar, which means your results will be less than satisfactory. Therefore, you will be farther from what it is you want. You want to do things for your body that make you feel good about who you are. It doesn't matter what you weigh. It only matters how you feel. If your clothes feel light and good on you, you feel great. You've got an air of confidence about you. But if your clothes feel tight, if you feel scrunched by your waistband, you're uncomfortable and aware of that uneasiness. If you are at all spiritual, you understand that your body is a gift from God. Are you treating it that way?

There are ten things you can do right now that will instantly and effectively increase your energy, improve your health, and keep your motor running.

1. Sleep

Getting enough sleep is essential to sustaining the energy you'll need for the six steps to living By Design. For some, it may be six hours, with a nap in the afternoon. For others, perhaps it's eight hours a night. If you're sleeping ten or more hours a day, you might as well get in the coffin and wait. No one who is living By Design is sleeping ten or more hours a night. Know how many hours is optimal for you, and then do whatever you can to sleep that many hours every night. If you didn't get your hours in, take a nap during the day. Many documented studies say napping is very productive.

A good night's sleep can help you look younger and feel better, boost your energy level, and keep you healthy. During sleep, our bodies release the greatest concentration of growth hormones (HGH), which help the body repair damaged tissue. When you're sick and the doctor tells you to go home and get some rest, what he is really saying is that rest and sleep are natural ways for the body to heal itself. Plain and simple, we function better in every area of our lives when we are well.

Yet I've had hundreds of nights where I've gotten little or not enough rest but still performed at a high level the next day. So if you don't get your hours in, don't allow that to be your excuse for living by default.

2. Eat for Energy

I have spent years conditioning myself and my mind to eat for one reason—energy. There is a strong connection between the types of foods you eat and the energy they supply. It's difficult to be at the top of your game if you haven't eaten enough of the right foods, or not eaten at all. The idea is to avoid foods that will spike your blood sugar. Rather, focus on the foods that maintain a steady level of energy throughout the day. My general rule is to eat five or six small meals a day, starting with a balanced breakfast in order to boost my energy and concentration. I usually have a midmorning protein shake or an energy bar, followed by a light lunch of salad and turkey or chicken. In the afternoon, if my energy level is slipping, I eat an apple or a banana or have another shake—just enough to keep my energy up from late afternoon through dinner. Avoid junk food because it causes havoc with blood sugar levels. Round out the day with a sensible dinner, but don't overindulge. The quality of your night's rest could be ruined by eating too much.

The major point I want to make is to eat for energy and not for comfort or out of habit or boredom or as a stress release. I promise you, when you make the transition to eating By Design, you'll be amazed at your newfound energy and how quickly your body will adapt to your new way of eating.

3. Hydrate

Aside from oxygen, water is the most essential component to our survival. Without it, the human body couldn't last for more than a few days. It would be similar to a car trying to run without gas. Every process in the body and all of our cell and organ functions would cease without water. It helps balance our body temperature, regulates metabolism, and forms the base for all bodily fluids. This is why it is so important to stay hydrated throughout the day.

Believe it or not, even a small decrease in our body's water content can bring about effects of mild dehydration, which can cause light-headedness, headaches, dizziness, and trouble focusing and staying awake, which can impair our ability to perform at our best and feel good throughout the day. It is important to drink water regularly in order to avoid daytime fatigue. Even though you may find it difficult to drink enough on a busy workday, try to keep a bottle of water handy at all times so hydration is always within arm's reach.

Diet soda, sweet teas, and other flavored drinks will not hydrate you. You need to drink at least forty-eight ounces of water a day to keep your body fully hydrated. For the next thirty days, stop drinking high-sugar or artificially sweetened drinks and replace them with plain water. Your body may detox from coming off all the sugar you've been consuming, but that discomfort will be temporary. Commit to thirty days and I promise you will notice a significant difference in your energy level and waistline.

4. Take Vitamins/Supplements

High energy comes from eating right every day. Hippocrates said, "Let food be your medicine and medicine be your food." Although I believe that the quality of the food we eat is essential to giving our body the vitamins and minerals it needs, it is virtually impossible and not always practical to ensure that everything we eat is as vitamin rich as it can be. Having enough iron in our diet is essential for energy, as is zinc, which affects the functioning of more than two hundred enzymes in the body. Most people do not get enough iron or zinc from food. Taking vitamins, minerals, and other supplements helps compensate for any deficiencies.

It's likely that your body needs a vitamin supplement if you are not getting enough nutrition from the food you eat. Either the foods lack the right vitamins, or your body is not absorbing them properly. The processing that most of our food goes through before it lands on our dinner plate can also reduce the original vitamin content. Vitamin deficiencies have been linked to overeating, eating too fast, indulging in late-night binges, consuming caffeine, smoking, and eating rich, greasy, spicy, and/or high-fat foods.

Vitamins are a form of preventative medicine, but they are not a cure-all. You still need to eliminate nutrient-poor foods from your diet and replace them with vitamin-rich, healthy, nutritious foods. Antioxidants are also important to help prevent cancer and heart disease. Antioxidants enhance your body's ability to fight off free radicals, which are unstable, hyperreactive atoms in your body that damage healthy cells and tissue. Vitamins C and E and beta-carotene are a few examples of antioxidants.

There are thousands of options when it comes to choosing vitamins and supplements that are right for your body. If you're confused about your particular needs, consult your physician or go to your local health foods store and share your goals so they can direct you to the right products for you.

5. Create an Exercise Plan

If you can't remember the last time you had a workout, a warning signal should be going off in your mind. There's no greater satisfaction for me than the exhaustion I feel after a good workout. I feel my best knowing I've left all I had to give on the field. Anytime I exert myself, I feel good. It doesn't have to be training in a gym. It can come from a rigorous walk, a run on the beach, even cleaning the house. There is a lot to be said for maintaining your flexibility, coordination, and strength. Exercise not only increases your muscle tone and metabolism, it also increases your energy, acts as a stress reducer, and strengthens your body's immune system.

If you don't have time for exercise in your busy schedule, *make* time. Get up an hour earlier. It may seem like a daunting task, but whether you realize it or not, it isn't difficult to design your own exercise routine. Focus on a program that is appropriate for your physical capabilities. Take the first step and work on something right away. Set out on a morning walk or jog and gradually build your way up. Do yoga, Pilates, strength training, or core workouts; join a gym or work out with a pal—the options are endless. Concentrate on exercises that revolve around the seven basic movements—pushing, pulling, lunging, bending, squatting, twisting, walking, or running— and you can't go wrong. In the end, your body and mind will thank you!

6. Be Active

Physical activity is an integral part of a healthy lifestyle. Exercise doesn't have to depend upon a fitness center or an expensive personal trainer. It may be easier, and more in your budget, to come up with a range of recreational activities that you enjoy doing daily or even weekly. Why not walk to a restaurant, the office, or the movies instead of driving or taking a cab?

My grandparents, who lived to be in their late eighties, walked three to five miles a day. When I asked Gramps why he did that, his answer was simple. "If you stop moving, you die." I never forgot his words. The bottom line is to get outside, be active, and move your body if you want to boost your energy.

7. Stand, Don't Sit

The human body is designed for movement and activity. Even though we may exercise, many of us sit most of the day, whether at our desk, in the office, or on the couch at home. Remaining sedentary contributes to weight gain, which also increases the risk of disease and sickness.

Hello!

Stand up!

Why not stand while making a business call at work? Look at what has happened to the human body because we go to work and we sit! I created something different in my workspace several years ago which I still practice today: I stand. And most of the people who work for me—whether in sales or client relations—have a stand-up work environment too. My team members tell me they feel better and the days go by faster because they are up, moving, and active. My advice is to look at your physical work environment and ask yourself how you can make it more conducive to standing. Perhaps you can elevate your computer keyboard or desk phone by placing it on top of a couple of boxes? Remove your chair and elevate your desk so it is comfortable and functional while you stand. If your co-workers think it is strange or different, I have two thoughts for you. First, who cares what they think? And second, this is a perfect opportunity to tell them why you're doing it and set a healthy example.

8. Create Flexibility

The sixth-century B.C. Chinese philosopher Lao-tzu said, "Softness and tenderness are attributes of life, and hardness and stiffness are attributes of death." If we want to stay fully alive, we must become tender, soft, and flexible. A flexible body and mind is fully alive.

Choosing to improve your physical flexibility will also improve your flexibility in other areas of your life. Rigid things tend to break; when you are limber, you can bend and adapt more easily to everything life throws at you. Whether it is an unexpected catastrophe or a spur-of-the-moment decision, you will be much more able to go with the flow. And your physical health affects the fitness of your mind.

How do you increase your flexibility? By regularly stretching. Spend fifteen minutes every day stretching your legs, lower back, and upper body. It can be as simple as arm circles, toe flexing at your desk, reaching down and touching your knees or toes, or a calf stretch while standing on a curb. If you want to be more energetic, practicing flexibility is a must.

9. Get Outside and Enjoy the Benefits of Sunlight and Fresh Air

Most people spend about 90 percent of their day indoors under artificial lighting while breathing stale air that has been endlessly circulated through heating and air-conditioning systems. If you think this doesn't have an effect on your body and mind, think again.

There is nothing like being in the great outdoors. Sun is the body's best source of vitamin D, which helps maintain the normal functioning of your nervous system, increases bone density, and promotes healthy bone growth. It is also essential to the body's absorption of calcium. Ten to fifteen minutes in the sun without sunscreen generates a day's worth of vitamin D. So be sure to get out from under any artificial lighting whenever you are able. Even if it is for only a few minutes on a lunch break.

And what would a bright sunny day be without a gentle breeze? "Stale" indoor air contains only positively charged atoms, whereas clean outdoor air is full of both positively and negatively charged atoms, which refresh your cells, improve your lung function, and kill bacteria and viruses in the air. Experiencing the benefits of nature is as easy as stepping out your front door.

10. Breathe

If you aren't breathing, you can be sure you aren't doing anything else. The process of simply inhaling and exhaling is more important than you may think. Your lungs take in air to supply your body with oxygen, which is vital for survival. Breathing also helps rid your body of toxins and waste products.

Breathing is controlled by your mood and state of mind. Controlling your breathing will help you gain more control over yourself. Have you ever taken a deep breath when you are angry or stressed out? This increase in oxygen to your body lowers your pulse rate and blood pressure. It may sound simple, but don't ignore the little things in life, especially breathing.

Many books have been written on the subjects of diet, exercise, health, and vitality. If you are committed to living your life By Design, changing your physical and dietary routines is essential for the energy you'll need to achieve all you desire. The ten simple disciplines outlined in this chapter will help you achieve the level of energy that I have every day. Your friends will want to know your secret. Tell them you've committed to energy, By Design.

CHAPTER

10

THE 5 EVOLUTIONS TO MASTER BY DESIGN LIVING

Allow me to take a moment to congratulate you for being well on your way to living By Design. I want to honor the hard work and fierce determination it will take to get you there. Believe me, it will be worth it.

Once you make the choice to live By Design, two things happen: Similar people, circumstances, opportunities, and information naturally gravitate to you. Like attracts like—it's a basic law of physics.

The second thing that happens is an understanding that you're not "bucking" the system; you're just living by your design. There may be resistance from naysayers and "defaulters" that your newfound ways are uncomfortable for them. Do not let this hold you back. Move through the world by setting the example that other people will want to live up to.

Once you realize that the system is working, you'll want to keep reinforcing your newfound way of life in everything you do. You will be amazed at how fast you can make the shift from living by default to By Design. Other people will begin to notice the changes you've made and inevitably want to do the same. We live in a society where most people look to others to make the changes we all want instead of taking action ourselves. As the old saying goes, "Sweep your front porch first and watch how others in the neighborhood respond." Although you may share a good book, a hot new restaurant, or a spectacular bottle of wine with your family, friends, colleagues, and neighbors, will you choose to share your secrets to living By Design? Choose to change your life and take notice of how living By Design affects those around you. Be the change you want to see in the world.

Now that you've got the fundamental principles, I want to leave you with something more that I know will help you master the process. I call these *The 5 Evolutions to Master By Design Living.* We all want mastery in our lives. We want to be fully engaged and present with every area that brings us success, wealth, and abundance. That is the epitome of living By Design. You're fully living your vision when you find yourself in action, allowing your life to be in a constant state of flow. You're loving the process and embracing the joy along the way. Enduring success comes from people who love what they do.

Persistence and practice are key to developing mastery in anything. Aikido Master George Leonard said, "Mastery is the mysterious process during which what is at first difficult becomes progressively easier and more pleasurable through practice." In Malcolm Gladwell's book *Outliers,* he says it takes ten thousand hours to become an expert at something. That's a little over four years! You cannot make a leap to "expert" without repetition and commitment. Fully living By Design is a process that will take longer than you want it to, although I assure you it won't be long before you see results. The more you practice, are persistent, and are fueled by passion, the quicker you will feel the effects of creating your life By Design.

The process you went through to get you here began when you became aware of what you wanted and declared that *this* was how you wanted your life to be. I call this the First Evolution of By Design Living. You made the choice for change by having a clear vision of what you are seeking by asking yourself the five fundamental questions discussed in Chapter 7. You'll find that the essence of what you want usually remains the same. How you choose to have it show up and in what form is usually where your answers differ throughout the evolution.

The Second Evolution is to get into massive action. Most businesses operate by looking at the year in four quarters. I believe that everything we do comes in ninety-day cycles. Most people quit in the last ten days of their ninety-day cycle. Here's something to remember so you don't give up. The ninety-day cycle is where you have to fall in love with the process, with the work to get you to your vision, and with whom you are becoming so you can eventually live By Design. You have to do all of the little things every day, especially the days you don't feel like doing them, to achieve your goal.

I cannot count the number of times someone has attended one of my seminars thinking their life is horrible, they've nothing going on and nothing to look forward to. They've resigned themselves to spending the rest of their days feeling miserable and helpless. Afterward, a lightbulb goes off. They get fired up and are excited by the possibilities, and then realize that this is going to be a lot of hard work. And they're the only person who can do the work if they want to reap the rewards. They slowly begin to do the things that bring them the power, but then they meet resistance from others around them who question why they're doing these things. These are the same people who can't wait to remind you that you've tried and failed in the past and there's no point in wasting time wishing for a better life. Right?

This is when you have to fight through other people's doubt and the four addictions and continue doing the things that bring you the power so you don't go back to where you started. More people fail in this stage than in any other evolution of mastering living By Design. Whatever you're aiming for, whether it's the reinvention of your relationship, a new business campaign, or getting into better physical shape, chunk everything you do into ninety-day cycles. You have to do the things that give you the power over and over again until you transform who you are. This takes massive commitment and a willingness to start over every time you hit a plateau or a setback until you get it right.

The Third Evolution to master is the Progression of Momentum. This is the phase where everything you do begins to pay off. The process gets easier and becomes more second nature than nurture. You suddenly recognize that the primary relationship in your life has improved. You find joy in the process. You're connecting with your kids, making more money, getting up in the morning and are excited to hit the gym . . . again. You realize that this is what living By Design feels like. What often happens in this phase, however, is that people think they have arrived and, as a result, they get lazy or complacent or simply stop trying. They celebrate their weight loss by going on an eating binge, driving themselves right back to the First Evolution. If this happens to you, you've got to get right back to the plan, recommit, and start a brand-new ninety-day cycle.

The Fourth Evolution is creating new structure and new accountabilities to stabilize your growth. If you don't reset and streamline your structure and accountability, you will not make it to the Fifth Evolution. To do this, you must create a new daily action checklist, refocus your intentions, change your gateway to gratitude, consider changing accountability partners, and alter your ten questions (see page 162) so that you can stabilize your new habits, visualizations, and everything else you have implemented into your new By Design living. If you don't reassess everything, you'll get bored, fall off, and potentially find yourself having to start the process all over again.

The fifth and final evolution is making the Extraordinary Leap. This is the phase where you no longer think about incremental growth in your life because living By Design is now a natural part of your daily routine. You no longer think about making your life merely better; you now expect and demand extraordinary. You wake up every morning with boundless energy, feeling full of joy. You radiate love, attraction, and tremendous possibility. After you've made the Extraordinary Leap, it is not uncommon to have to go back and reshape, restructure, and restabilize your vision and plan to maintain your newfound enlightened state.

When I first decided to write this book, I ran my platform and program past my literary agent, Dan. He's a practical and savvy guy whose opinion I greatly respect. He listened carefully as I methodically laid out my plan on how I have been helping people achieve success, abundance, joy, and fulfillment in their lives. After I finished my presentation, I paused, looked at Dan, and asked, "What do you think?"

He didn't say a word.

Uh-oh, I thought.

Perhaps he could see the worried look in my eyes that, somewhere around a minute or two into my speech, I lost the guy. And then he said something I'll never forget. "Living By Design sounds hard." I laughed because he was right. I looked him square in the eyes and said, "If it were easy, everyone would be living an extraordinary life."

Living By Design takes hard work and a willingness to dig deep into your heart, mind, and soul so you can finally let go of all the burdens that have been weighing you down and holding you back from achieving everything you dream of having. Now more than ever, don't you deserve to have those things in your life? It's time to roll up your sleeves and embrace the boundless opportunities that are right in front of you.

We can't control the uncertainty in our lives, but we can take control of our physical, spiritual, mental, financial, and professional self by the way we respond to circumstances. This is how you will know you're living By Design.

Whenever you're feeling uncertain or frustrated, remember to not allow yourself to doubt the process, especially if it's not working the way you want it to right now. Be sure to stay in the joy of your inspired action. Doing this will keep you from going back to living with the four addictions—or, worse, living by default. By seeing the positive in your everyday activities, you'll be focused on what's working and not what is missing.

To help you stay connected to your vision, look for confirmation—signs that you are on the right path. Continually look for proof (and it will be there for you to see) that your vision has become a reality, that you're achieving everything you want, and that it's all working out.

A few years ago, I taught my kids a game to show them how the universe always delivers. The premise is that money is everywhere and ever flowing if they're looking for it. So when they see a penny on the ground, they pick it up. I tell them to thank the universe and say, "Money is easy and everywhere." Finding the penny is their sign that money is, in fact, everywhere. Some people see the penny, while others walk right on by.

Have you ever thought about buying a new car and then suddenly noticed that the car is everywhere you go? That vision is you tuning in to what you want. If you want to receive messages from the universe, you've got to tune in to the right frequency for proof. Messages are everywhere if you are ready and open and have the desire to receive them. Tuning in is as simple as noticing and allowing the signs to show up that reinforce that you are on the right track. It's being receptive to and accepting of the possibilities.

Proof can come anytime, anyplace. I've gone to the movies where a character on-screen says something I've been thinking about. I've walked into a bookstore and put my hands on a book that delivers a message I needed to get. Soon, you will have these same experiences. You will be amazed at their frequency and accuracy.

Finding the proof is a game changer. It is validation and confirmation—which everyone needs to reinforce their actions. Think of this as the universe or some higher power patting you on the back and saying, "*Atta* boy, *atta* girl. Keep up the good work. You're on the right path."

We live in a world full of choices. Everything we do is a choice. We choose to go to work—or not; choose to return a phone call—or not; choose to be calm, present, and in the moment—or not; choose to say "I love you"—or not. When you're living By Design, you become more aware of the impact of these choices and therefore begin to make better decisions every day.

Now that you've made it to the end of my book, will you choose to change? Go back to our original exercise on choosing to change in Chapter 7 (page 130).

What are the benefits of doing so and the consequences of not?

I know that some people out there will live the rest of their lives believing they have no choices. They think where they were born or how they were raised or where they went to school will dictate the outcome of their lives. Those people use their circumstances as a reflection of how their life has to be. I have met countless people who came from nothing and, because of the power of choice, were able to alter their reality and make their lives successful and full of love and joy.

I met a young man a couple of years ago named Rudy Garcia-Tolson, who was born with a birth defect that left him with two nonfunctioning legs. By the time he was five years old, Rudy had endured fifteen operations before deciding to have his legs amputated above the knee. His legs didn't work and he was tired of being in a wheelchair or crawling on the ground, so he told his mother he'd rather lose his legs than continue living as he was. All Rudy wanted was to run and play like the other kids his age.

Eventually, Rudy started changing the perception of what someone missing his legs could accomplish. When he was sixteen, he swam in the 200-meter individual medley in two minutes forty-two seconds to take home the Paralympic Gold Medal from Athens in 2004. He went even faster in Beijing, shaving five full seconds off his time to win his second gold medal and shatter his own world record. He has run a mile in under six minutes and has been showcased around the world. Rudy is an awesome example of someone who made the choice to change. The next time you think you "can't," think of Rudy or Ben Comen. If change was possible for them, what is possible for you?

Knowing what you now know about living by default versus living By Design, what will you choose to do with the rest of your life? Will you continue being a victim, choosing to live as you always have, or will you become the victor who chooses the inspired path?

If you still have doubts, *doubt all the stories and garbage you've been feeding yourself for years!* Wake up and go for extraordinary! When you were born, do you think there was a sign on your back that said, "Go be ordinary and average, and suffer"? Or did it say, "You are a child of mine. Go be extraordinary!"

My final question for you is this: Have you been living up to your end of the deal?

Most people have not because of conditioning and the environment in which they live. This is your chance to break out of the mold that you've been living in. More important, you're not doing this just for yourself.

Do it for your family and loved ones.

Do it for the people you work with, your friends, and your neighbors.

Do it for all the people who told you at one time or another that you couldn't.

Most important, do it for you, my friend.

Welcome to *your* life, By Design!

ACKNOWLEDGMENTS

There are so many people I want to acknowledge who helped bring the vision of this book to life.

I have to start by thanking my friend Toni Haber who introduced me to the most extraordinary writer and partner, Laura Morton. Laura captured my voice on the page in a way that preserved my authenticity and exuberant style—a skill I can only describe as truly By Design. I owe a big thank you to my agent Dan Conaway of Writers House for believing in my vision. Even though Dan thought my ideas sounded hard, he stood firm in his conviction that I had to write this book for all the people out there living by default. Thanks also to Adam Mitchell for being the ultimate writer's assistant. There's no way we could have done this book without your dedication and help.

I want to thank my incredible, dynamic, and supportive team at Ballantine Books, including my publisher, Libby McGuire, and my fantastic editor, Luke Dempsey, who got my message from the very start. It has been a journey that I know is the start of something big. And to the rest of the people who made this book possible, including Theresa Zoro, Kim Hovey, Sanyu Dillon, Cindy Murray, Kristin Fessler, Katie O'Callaghan, Ryan Doherty, and many others.

I want to thank all the people who have assisted, coached, and consulted with me over the last twenty years. Each of you have made such an indelible impact on my life; the late Jim Rohn, Mike Vance, Ron Arden, Theresa Jabbour, Tony Robbins, Brian Tracy, Jim Marks,

Gary Vaynerchuk, T. Harv Eker, and Mark Victor Hansen. These are just a few of the inspirational leaders who helped me learn, grow, and become a better coach.

I especially want to thank Bill Mitchell, my friend and mentor, for always being there and for your unwavering belief and guidance.

Thank you to my team at Tom Ferry-yourcoach for always supporting me. Steve Belmonte for always having my back; Biagio Mancini, for being my voice of reason while I keep dreaming big; Lauren Johns for being my biggest cheerleader and best secret marketing weapon; Debbie Holloway, the general and queen of GSD; my sales team; client relations; KG and the internal team who make it all happen! And to our incredible coaches, trainers, and consultants . . . you make it possible for so many to live By Design. There are no words to let you all know how grateful I am for that.

There would be no TFYC without our clients: You have taught me so much throughout the years. Together we have forged a path that has led us to the articulation of the message in this book. Although the list is too big to include each of you by name, I have to give a special shout-out to my original ten clients of TFYC, who believed in me enough to jump aboard the train before it ever pulled out of the station. Maxine and Marti Gellens, Carole and Genelle Geronsin, Laura Dandoy, Stephen Christie, Lori Newman, Ty Leon Guererro, Joe DiRaffelle, and Grace Sergio.

And to the rest of our clients over the years—you know who you are—thank you all, including my personal clients, Inner Circle, and all of the coaching and consulting clients of our firm, for allowing us to support you in your greatness!

I want to thank Chad Cooper, Claude Yacole, Jay Talley, Kirk Kessel, Thach Nguyen, and Rick Kurtz for your friendship, for hearing out my crazy ideas, for supporting each others' visions, and for all the fun we have.

All my friends on Facebook, Twitter, and YouTube, who will help take my message global. I am so appreciative for all of your support and inspiration.

To my family, Mom, Pete, Dad, Grandma Liz, Michelle, Ron, Patrick, Matthew, Claudine, Ragen, Pua, Tony, Lola, John, Joe, and Brie: Your encouragement and guidance has been unwavering, and for that I remain now and forever grateful.

And finally, to my amazing and loving wife, Kathy, and our sons, Michael and Steven. Without you, none of this would be possible.

ABOUT THE AUTHOR

TOM FERRY is a business coach and life strategist with a particular emphasis on real estate and related industries. He is also CEO of YourCoach, a multimillion-dollar full-service sales and marketing business. He leads more than two hundred business motivation seminars per year across the United States, whereby he introduces fifty thousand new people a year to his message.

LAURA MORTON has co-authored numerous *New York Times* bestsellers, working with the Jonas Brothers, Duane "Dog" Chapman, and Melissa Etheridge, among many others.

ABOUT THE TYPE

The text of this book was set in Legacy, a typeface family designed by Ronald Arnholm and issued in digital form by ITC in 1992. Both its serifed and unserifed versions are based on an original type created by the French punchcutter Nicholas Jenson in the late fifteenth century. While Legacy tends to differ from Jenson's original in its proportions, it maintains much of the latter's characteristic modulations in stroke.

FREE LIFE! BY DESIGN SUPPORT TOOLS

Want to benefit more from the ideas in my book?

I've created five essential resources inspired by my book that will help you put "Life! By Design" ideas into practice!

Visit www.TomFerry.com/Resources
and register to receive these free gifts from me!

1 Life! By Design Video

Get access to this 30-minute video hosted by me to help you put my "Life! By Design" ideas into practice.

2 Life! By Design Coaching Call Session

Receive a private one-on-one coaching call session with a Tom Ferry–trained Life! By Design consultant.

3 Life! By Design Daily Gratitude Journal

Download my Gratitude Journal to start your mornings off By Design.

4 Life! By Design Coaching Lessons

Receive membership to my exclusive weekly coaching lessons delivered electronically to your email in-box.

5 Life! By Design Vision Board

Download my step-by-step guide to creating your Life! By Design.

After you've received these valuable tools, connect with me on Twitter at @CoachTomFerry and on Facebook at Facebook.com/CoachTomFerry to share your progress and keep me updated!

Strategy Matters and Passion Rules!

Tom Ferry